DISCARD

The New
Enchantment of America
MISSISSIPPI

By Allan Carpenter

CHILDRENS PRESS, CHICAGO

ACKNOWLEDGMENTS

For assistance in the preparation of the revised edition, the author thanks:
DR. ROBERT L. ROBINSON, Executive Director and MRS. JEAN MAY, Public Affairs
Department, Mississippi Agricultural and Industrial Board.

American Airlines—Anne Vitaliano, Director of Public Relations; *Capitol Historical Society*,
Washington, D. C.; *Newberry Library,* Chicago, Dr. Lawrence Towner, Director; *Northwestern University Library*, Evanston, Illinois; *United Airlines*—John P. Grember, Manager
of Special Promotions; Joseph P. Hopkins, Manager, News Bureau.

UNITED STATES GOVERNMENT AGENCIES: *Department of Agriculture*—Robert Hailstock, Jr.,
Photography Division, Office of Communication; Donald C. Schuhart, Information Divi-
sion, Soil Conservation Service. *Army*—Doran Topolosky, Public Affairs Office, Chief of
Engineers, Corps of Engineers. *Department of Interior*—Louis Churchville, Director of
Communications; EROS Space Program—Phillis Wiepking, Community Affairs; Charles
Withington, Geologist; Mrs. Ruth Herbert, Information Specialist; Bureau of Reclama-
tion; National Park Service—Fred Bell and the individual sites; Fish and Wildlife Service—
Bob Hines, Public Affairs Office. *Library of Congress*—Dr. Alan Fern, Director of the
Department of Research; Sara Wallace, Director of Publications; Dr. Walter W. Ristow,
Chief, Geography and Map Division; Herbert Sandborn, Exhibits Officer. *National
Archives*—Dr. James B. Rhoads, Archivist of the United States; Albert Meisel, Assistant
Archivist for Educational Programs; David Eggenberger, Publications Director; Bill Leary,
Still Picture Reference; James Moore, Audio-Visual Archives. *United States Postal Serv-
ice*—Herb Harris, Stamps Division.

For assistance in the preparation of the first edition, the author thanks:
Consultant Laura D.S. Harrell, Research Assistant, Department of Archives and History,
State of Mississippi; Governor Paul B. Johnson; A.P. Bennett, Director, Division of
Instruction, Department of Education, State of Mississippi.

Illustrations on the preceding pages:
Cover photograph: Mississippi riverboat,
James R. Rowan
Page 1: Commemorative stamps of historic
interest
Page 2-3: Vicksburg area, Department of
the Army, Lower Mississippi Valley
Division, Corps of Engineers
Page 3: (Map) USDI Geological Survey
Pages 4-5: Vicksburg area, EROS Space
Photo, USDI Geological Survey, EROS
Data Center

Project Editor, Revised Edition:
  Joan Downing
Assistant Editor, Revised Edition:
  Mary Reidy

**Library of Congress Cataloging in
Publication Data**

Carpenter, John Allan, 1917-
  Mississippi.

  (His The new enchantment of America)
  SUMMARY: A presentation of the
Magnolia State, including its history,
resources, famous citizens, and places of
interest.
  1. Mississippi—Juvenile literature.
  [1. Mississippi] I. Title.
  II. Series: Carpenter, John Allan,
1917-   The new enchantment of America.
F341.3.C3 1978 976.2 78-3400
ISBN 0-516-04124-X

CONTENTS

William Faulkner, a leading twentieth-century author, wove the history and tradition of the South into his writings.

A True Story to Set the Scene

A ROMANTIC ANCESTOR

The long shadows of the trees were beginning to slant across the street. Night was coming, and the boy did not know where to go or what to do. Tired after an extremely long walk, he sat down on the steps of the hotel at Pontotoc and burst into tears. As he wept bitterly, "a girl came along and inquired the cause of his distress," as he later described the scene himself. "Having learned the facts . . . she promptly went and obtained the money to pay his hotel bill and gave it to him."

Drying his tears, the boy is said to have resolved that some day he would do two things. The story of that boy and that girl and of what happened to his resolves is one of the many stories of enchantment of Mississippi. In that story is much that is typical of the Magnolia State—the elegance and spirit of the aristocracy, the genius of business and letters, the bravery of war, the legends of dueling and violence, and, over all, the feeling of romance.

The boy was William C. Falkner. He had walked the nearly 200 miles (about 322 kilometers) from Middleton, Tennessee, to Pontotoc to make his home with his uncle T. I. Word. When he reached Pontotoc he found that Word had left for Aberdeen the day before. The story persists that on his first unhappy day in Pontotoc he still had the spirit to resolve that someday he would marry the girl who had helped him, and that along the route he had just covered on foot he would build a railroad over which he could ride in style. Whether or not the story of the vows is correct, Falkner did marry the girl, and did build the railroad.

Falkner moved to Ripley and made his home with another uncle, J. W. Thompson. The story of Falkner's first financial success is a strange one. He was a member of the posse which captured an outlaw, A. J. McCannon. Among McCannon's crimes was the robbery and brutal murder of a family of four.

As a part-time cleanup boy at the jail, Falkner was able to talk with the man and get his story. He wrote a pamphlet called *The Life and*

Confessions of A. J. McCannon. According to a friend of Falkner, on the day McCannon was executed, Falkner "deposited the pamphlets on the stand erected for the gallows and commenced selling them. The atrocity of the murder had attracted an immense crowd. The demand was so great for the books at a dollar apiece that every hour or two Falkner had to go to his hotel to deposit his money. He returned to Memphis the next day, paid Gurion (who had allowed him to publish the pamphlet on credit) and since then has never wanted a dollar."

Falkner studied under a local schoolteacher, and was taught law by his uncle. He served in the war with Mexico. After the war he began to practice law in Ripley, in partnership with his uncle. Falkner later became a prosperous planter.

When the tragedy of civil war reached the Ripley area, Falkner became a hero by aiding General Nathan Bedford Forrest in the defense of Ripley. Times were hard in Ripley after the war, just as they were throughout Mississippi, but the legend persists that Colonel William C. Falkner never forgot his second boyhood vow.

Eventually the tracks began to stretch out toward Tennessee. Colonel Falkner was keeping his promise to build a railroad. Finally the Colonel's line ran clear to Middleton, Tennessee, and connected there with the Memphis-Charleston line. He called the road Ripley, Ship Island & Kentucky. Later he extended it southward, and it became the Gulf, Mobile & Northern. William Falkner, no longer a boy, could now ride in style over the long miles that had so tired him when he first walked to Mississippi.

As a high-spirited and hot tempered Southern gentleman, Colonel Falkner often had settled his quarrels with duels, it has been said. When he ran for the state legislature in 1899, his opponent was Colonel R. J. Thurmond, at one time an associate of Falkner in the railroad business and a good friend. The former friends quarreled bitterly when Falkner beat Thurmond in the election, and Thurmond challenged Falkner to a duel.

Falkner refused. He said he already had killed too many people through dueling, and he had no inclination to kill his former friend. On the day of his second election to the legislature, Colonel William

C. Falkner was walking down a street of Ripley when Colonel Thurmond stepped up and fatally shot him. In the Ripley cemetery, a marble shaft marks Falkner's grave.

William C. Falkner was not only a lawyer, planter, war veteran, railroad builder, and legislator, but also a well-known author. His works include *Reply to Uncle Tom's Cabin, The Little Brick Church,* and *Rapid Ramblings in Europe.* However, his most famous and controversial work was *The White Rose of Memphis.* This novel shocked William C. Falkner's neighbors and friends in Mississippi, and it may have been a forecast of things to come when Colonel Falkner's great-grandson would shock another generation of Mississippians with his novel *Sanctuary.* This author once again was a William, who now spelled his name Faulkner and who brought to Mississippi a genius for writing that has been called "one of the greatest in American history."

So skillfully in his writing did William Faulkner reconstruct the lives of his great-grandfather and of other members of his family and of his home state that they have become familiar to people the world around.

Rowan Oak, William Faulkner's house

Dunns Falls

Lay of the Land

"MEACT CHASSIPI"

The state of Mississippi is dominated by the great river from which it takes its name, and yet it has an important western river boundary that has no connection with the Mississippi River. The state is one of the Gulf states, and yet the longest portion of its southern boundary is considerably removed from the Gulf of Mexico. These are only two of the many seeming contradictions and unusual features which add interest to the physical layout of the state of Mississippi.

By far the most prominent feature of the geography is the mighty river called Meact Chassipi by the Indians, roughly translated as "Ancient Father of Waters." For 400 miles (about 644 kilometers) along the state's western boundary, the mighty Mississippi River swells and courses, ebbs and flows, gleams and glistens, twists and turns.

The "surprise boundary" of the state is the Pearl River, which forms about 75 miles (about 121 kilometers) of the second river dividing line between Mississippi and Louisiana. Other neighboring states are Arkansas, Tennessee, and Alabama. The far southern boundary of the state of Mississippi is formed by Mississippi Sound, a sheltered portion of the Gulf of Mexico, which provides the state with a coastline 202 miles (about 325 kilometers) long. A row of barrier islands—Cat, Ship, Horn, and Petit Bois—shelters Mississippi Sound from the sometimes stormy waters of the Gulf of Mexico.

A quick glance at the map might give the impression that there are no other natural boundaries of the state. However, the northeast corner, instead of coming together in a right angle, is cut off by a ragged boundary line where the Tennessee River juts a small elbow into Mississippi. The remaining boundaries are man-made—a straight northern boundary with Tennessee, an equally straight boundary between northeast Louisiana and southwest Mississippi, and a very long boundary with Alabama, which appears to be straight but is not quite. It veers off slightly to the east where the boundary between Clark and Wayne counties meets the Alabama border.

PHYSICAL DESCRIPTION

The state of Mississippi is divided into ten main areas, each having a distinct physical characteristic; known as physiographic regions.

The general impression held by those not familiar with Mississippi is that it is almost completely flat. However, this is far from the case. Only the Alluvial Plain is level. Of Mississippi's total 47,716 square mile (123,584 square kilometers) area, the most pronounced physical feature is this vast Alluvial Plain area, known as the Mississippi Delta region. Its main portion extends about 200 miles (about 322 kilometers) from the meeting of the Mississippi and Yazoo rivers to the boundary with Tennessee. Averaging about 65 miles (about 105 kilometers) wide, the Delta contains some of the richest land in the world. At one time the region was under the waters of an arm of the Gulf of Mexico, then slowly was filled in by particles of soil brought by the Mississippi and other rivers.

On the eastern edge of the Delta is a line of hills ranging from 5 to 15 miles (about 8 to 24 kilometers) in width. At one time these hills formed the shoreline of the ancient Gulf. Their scientific name is loess hills, but they are known popularly as the Bluff Hills. South of Vicksburg a narrow extension of the Delta extends between the Bluff Hills and the Mississippi River.

Eastward from the Bluff Hills, a region known as the Brown Loam reaches from the Tennessee border to the Louisiana border on the south. The soil of this region was brought in and deposited by the winds, which carried it from northern regions where the rocks were being ground to dust by the succeeding glaciers. Actually the soil of the Brown Loam region is a layer of rock dust from 30 to 90 feet (about 9 to 27 meters) deep, very rich in plant food.

The extreme southern portion of the Mississippi panhandle is made up of a region known as the Gulf Coastal Meadows, or the Coastal Plain Meadows, ranging from 5 to 15 miles (about 8 to 24 kilometers) in width. The gently rolling surface is generally level and usually not much above sea level. However, the highest elevations on the coast between Corpus Christi, Texas, and Pensacola, Florida, are the Pine Hills, near Deslisle.

One of the largest physiographic regions in Mississippi is the Longleaf Pine Belt, generally known as the Piney Woods. This occupies much of the southern half of the state and at one time was blanketed by virgin longleaf yellow pine; now large areas of it have been reforested. Here the soil is red and yellow sandy loam.

To the north is the thin stretch of the Jackson Prairie Belt, a district of rolling land in which numbers of small prairies are found. Its black calcareous soil offers fine farming opportunities.

Immediately north of the Jackson Prairie Belt are the North Central Hills, a yellowish-brown loam mixed with silt and clay. This loam ranges from 2 to 15 feet (about .6 to 4 meters) thick.

Enclosing the northeast corner of the state is the Flatwoods Region, a thin stretch of flat land, sweeping in a half-moon around the remaining regions—the Black Prairie, Pontotoc Ridge, and Tennessee River Hills.

Pontotoc Ridge stretches in the form of a wedge for about 150 miles (about 241 kilometers), touching the western border of the Black Prairie. The soil is made up of rich sandy loam.

The rough Tennessee River Hills make up the northeastern corner of Mississippi. Although not mountains, they rise to an average altitude of 650 feet (about 198 meters). Woodall Mountain, 806 feet (about 246 meters), is the highest point in the state. The hills are composed of red, sandy loam liberally mixed with pebbles.

A scythe-shaped sweep of land around the west border of the Tennessee River Hills is the Black Prairie Region. This is a change from the hill country. Its smoothly rolling surface is covered with grass most of the year. The soil is clay loam—black, calcareous, good for dairying and farming. The Black Prairie is lower than the eastern hills; the northern part reaches about 400 feet (about 122 meters); the surface falls southward to about 179 feet (about 55 meters).

RIVERS AND LAKES

Mississippi is one of the few states where there is a three-way divide of the waters. This point is near Iuka. Water falling on the

The mighty Mississippi is studied in model form at the Corps of Engineers Waterways Experiment Station, Vicksburg.

north and east side of this point flows into the Tennessee River system, coursing north until it meets the Ohio River, then back down the Mississippi past the western border of the state where it originated. Water on the south and east of the divide flows to the Gulf by way of the Tombigbee, Pascagoula, and Pearl river systems. Water on the west of the divide flows into the rivers that enter the Mississippi River directly on the state's western boundary. The largest of these are the Yazoo, Big Black, and Homochitto rivers.

According to legend, the name Yazoo means River of Death in the Indian language; it has also been translated as meaning "leaf." As the River of Death, it takes its name from an Indian battle in which many braves were killed. The Yazoo drains much of the northwestern third of Mississippi, through tributaries such as the Sunflower, Coldwater, Tallahatchie, and Yalobusha.

The Leaf and Chickasawhay rivers come together not many miles from the Gulf to form the Pascagoula, known picturesquely as the "Singing River." The strange singing sound, resembling the buzzing of a flight of bees, is heard best in the warm months, toward evening. No one has ever been able to determine just what causes the strange but pleasant sound—possibly the rustle of the water over a pebbly bottom, the noise of fish, or the sucking of currents over holes in the bottom.

Indian legend explains the singing river: Two tribes went to war over an Indian princess who married into an opposing tribe. When

16

the battle turned against the young chief and his bride, the couple and his people all walked into the river and committed suicide. According to the legend, the singing of the river is their song of death as it rises eternally from the depths of the waters.

The Tombigbee River rises in Mississippi, as do some of its tributaries, but the largest part of its course flows through Alabama. The Indian word Tombigbee means a "coffin maker."

Other rivers of Mississippi include the Hobolochitto, Chunky, Luxapalila, Bogue Chitto, Buttahatchie, and Tallahaga.

Other watercourses of the state are slow-moving waterways known as bayous. Sometimes these connect two rivers, sometimes a river and a lake; sometimes they connect rivers or lakes with the Gulf. Cassidy Bayou is the longest in Mississippi.

Inland water of Mississippi covers 493 square miles (1,277 square kilometers). Natural lakes are mostly those formed whenever the Mississippi River took another course and left an unconnected loop of water to create a lake. Some of these are known as horseshoe lakes, because they were formed in what once were great horseshoe-shaped bends of the river. Lake Cormorant, Moon Lake, Lake Washington, and Eagle Lake are good examples of these.

The largest lakes of the state are artificial, formed by damming the waters of the many rivers. Among the major reservoirs of Mississippi are Grenada, Enid, Sardis, Arkabutla, Ross R. Barnett, and Pickwick, the last shared with Alabama and Tennessee, and formed from the Tennessee River by Pickwick Dam in Tennessee.

IN ANCIENT TIMES

Over periods of hundreds of millions of years, the surface of what is now Mississippi was sometimes covered by seas and on other occasions was partly out of the water. When the seas prevailed, tremendous amounts of shells accumulated on the ocean bottoms to form limestone; in later periods plant life grew and then when the seas came once more, the plants were buried deeper and deeper, forming carbonaceous materials. Sandstone, ochre, clays, chalk, lignite, and

17

other materials were formed in numerous layers of the earth, as the seas came and went.

Eventually, pressures below the earth's surface raised huge mountains, known as the ancient Appalachians. In the millions of years that followed, these were worn completely level by the slow but certain action of wind and water. Once again seas covered the area, depositing more layers of limestone, sandstone, green sand marls, and shale, as time and again the muddy bottom of the sea under great pressure was compressed into stone.

Once more the land was raised, the seas departed for the last time, and mountains were formed. Then again the forces of wind and rain and flowing waters ate at the once tremendous heights until they were worn down to the Appalachian Mountains we know today. The present hills of northeastern Mississippi are extensions of these mountains, some of the oldest highlands remaining in the world.

Much later, the present Delta region still remained under the waters of a bay which extended as far north as Cairo, Illinois. Over the vast stretches of time, the rivers carried soils, sands, and rocks from the regions as far north as Minnesota, from the slopes of the Rockies as far west as Montana, and from the northeast as far as New York State. Gradually, the shallow bay was filled in by the great ancient Mississippi River, which kept extending its own length as it built up its delta. This process is still going on, as the delta land continues to build up territory at its mouth.

The glaciers that covered the northern regions had no direct effect on Mississippi, but when they melted, the tremendous load of water and silt carried by the rivers hastened the delta-building process. The rivers that carved the huge flood from glaciers were bigger than they are at present, and their former banks are visible as bluffs, sometimes far from the present lower river banks. Some of the banks and cliffs, however, were formed by loess—wind-carried materials.

Another effect of the glaciers occurred when the icy covering made it impossible for anything to live in the north. Many new creatures were forced to come down into Mississippi.

For hundreds of millions of years, animal and plant life have thrived in present-day Mississippi. Most of the animal fossil remains that have been found are those of sea creatures—innumerable kinds of shellfish, and even a creature somewhat resembling whales. Growing to 70 or 80 feet (21 or 24 meters) in length, these were known as zeuglodons, and in Mississippi their vertebrae have been found, measuring as long as 16 inches (about 41 centimeters). Among the more interesting plant fossils of Mississippi are those of the petrified forest at Flora, where there are enormous "logs" dating back millions of years.

CLIMATE

Mississippi's climate has been described by the state's Agricultural and Industrial Board as "mild, with seasonal variations. It permits maximum opportunities for pleasant living and productive work and has played an important role in attracting both industry and tourists to the state.

"Industry has found that in Mississippi certain construction and storage problems commonly encountered in colder climates are eliminated and that lost-time and absenteeism due to severe weather are extremely rare. Other advantages offered by Mississippi's climate include: simplified heating and cooling considerations, improved transportation schedules, increased opportunities for outdoor recreation, and improved morale."

The annual average temperature ranges from 63°F (17.2°C) in the cooler more northern division of the state to around 68°F (20°C) in the warmer southern divisions. Killing frosts generally reach the Tupelo area in October; they come to the Woodville region in mid-November and do not reach the Gulf Coast until December. The state as a whole is freeze-free from 200 to 270 days per year, while some places may have as few as 11 days of freezing weather in a year.

Rainfall varies from north to south. Mean annual precipitation ranges from about 51 inches (about 130 centimeters) in the northern areas to around 62 inches (about 157 centimeters) in the coastal division. During the winter most precipitation centers in the north, with a minimum on the coast.

Footsteps on the Land

MOUNDS OF EVIDENCE

The great river rose higher and higher, flooding the entire countryside. Raised above the flood waters was a small island, on which a crowd of dark-skinned people huddled; babies cried; dogs barked; there was fear and confusion, but they were safe from the awful waters, thanks to their foresight in raising a tall mound of earth that would extend above the highest flood.

The people were some of the prehistoric peoples of the state of Mississippi. The mounds made by these prehistoric peoples are still widely scattered about the state. Authorities are only guessing when they say some of the highest of these were made to provide a place of safety during floods, but the guess seems to be a good one.

The ancient peoples had many other uses for these mounds, which are the main evidence that people lived in the region hundreds and thousands of years before written records were kept. The mounds were made for several purposes. Some of them provided high places from which signals could be sent; others served as elevated foundations for important buildings or temples; some were used for fortifications; some of the mounds were simply refuse heaps on which wastes were deposited or shells were piled high; probably more mounds were used for burial places than any other single purpose.

One of the most impressive relics of prehistoric inhabitants in Mississippi is found near where the Sunflower River enters Lake George. Known as Mound Place, this was apparently a village with a heavy wall fortification around it. Within the wall of earth are 25 mounds, all grouped around a principal mound. This looms almost 60 feet (about 18 meters) high, and the whole fortified area can be viewed from its top. The square base of the principal mound covers almost 2 acres (about .8 hectares), and its top is only somewhat less than a fourth of the base.

Winterville Mounds

21

The largest of the Mississippi state mounds is Selsertown Mound (also called Emerald Mound), not far from the village of Washington. This pyramid-shaped mound is only artificial, but its base extends about 600 feet (about 183 meters) in length and 400 feet (about 122 meters) in width, covering about 6 acres (about 2.4 hectares). Many items that belonged to ancient peoples have been excavated from it.

The state of Mississippi is rich in these mounds, particularly in the north and west and along the Mississippi River. Another important cluster of mounds is the Winterville group. A central mound rises to more than 55 feet (about 17 meters), and 14 smaller ones surround it. The largest shell mound found anywhere on the state's coast is that near Deslisle, testifying to the prehistoric peoples' hearty appetite for shellfish. In the state have been found many stone implements made by prehistoric people using the processes of polishing, grinding, or chipping. These include axes, agricultural implements such as spades and hoes, mortars and pestles for grinding grain and stone, cups and bowls, and other items.

Among the most interesting stones are those known as "discoidal" or chunky stones. Many of these stones were carved, sometimes quite skillfully, to represent animals or people. Some of the most remarkable of these carvings were made on calumets, known as pipes of peace, many of which have been found in Mississippi. These were very sacred objects, and much time was spent in making them from pottery or carving them elaborately from stone.

FROM NATCHEZ TO CHOCTAW TO CHICKASAW

At the beginning of recorded history, three major Indian groups occupied present-day Mississippi. There may have been as many as thirty thousand Indians living in the area at that time, one of the largest Indian populations in the present-day United States. The largest of these groups was the Choctaw, whose ancestral grounds covered much of the southern half of the state and extended on into present-day Alabama. The Chickasaw lived in the northern part of the state, and the Natchez made their home along the Mississippi River. All three of these groups were part of the great Muskogean language stock.

Smaller groups also lived in the region of present Mississippi. On the upper Yazoo River, Taposa, Chakchiuma, and Ibitoupa groups formed a buffer between the constantly warring Chickasaw and Choctaw. These smaller groups were of related Muskogean stock. Relatives of the Choctaw, the Pascagoula and Acolopissa, made their home in the region of what is now the Pascagoula River. Tunica, Koroa, Tiou, Grigra, and Yazoo lived along the lower stretches of the river which took its name from the last group.

The Biloxi lived on the Gulf Coast, and the Dog people (Ofo), living north on the Yazoo, were related to the Sioux, or Dakota, more commonly found in the north and west of the United States.

All of these Indians except the Choctaw were considered to be exceptional people physically. The Natchez, particularly, were tall, generally over 6 feet (1.82 meters), and nearly perfect in body build. An early writer said, "There was not a man among them who was either overloaded with flesh, or almost completely deprived of this necessary appendage to the body." Of the Mississippi Indians in general, early historian J. F. H. Claiborne wrote, "They were tall, well developed, active with classic features and intellectual expressions; they were grave, haughty, deliberate and always self-possessed."

The Choctaw were not so tall; however, the practice of flattening the head by fastening a heavy sandbag on the heads of babies probably served to reduce their height. Choctaw were not quite as remarkable physically as the other Indians of Mississippi.

Each morning as the sun rose over the major village of the Natchez on St. Catherine's Creek in present-day Adams County, the leader of the Natchez would come out of his house and salute his celestial brother, the rising sun, by giving a long yell and three puffs on his calumet (peace pipe). This sacred ruler was the Great Sun, representative of the Sun itself, which was worshiped by the Natchez. His house on a mound in the center of the village faced east so that he could easily carry out his morning ritual.

In some ways the mother of this great chief was even more powerful than her son. Having the title of Woman Chief, she held the authority of life and death and was much honored, but she seldom used her authority.

Natchez noblemen and women had a language that was entirely different from that of the lower class, who were known as Stinkards. The women spoke the language of the noblemen but used a completely distinctive pronunciation from that of the men. When one Frenchman tried to learn the language, he took the pronunciation of the women, and a contemptuous brave remarked, "Since thou hast the pretensions to be a man, why dost thou lisp like a woman?"

The Chickasaw villages were built along a single street; sometimes villages would be strung out down one road and formed almost a connected settlement for their entire length. One of the greatest of these villages was Long Town, stretching for miles (kilometers) along the crest of Pontotoc Ridge. The war-loving Chickasaw had made these villages so strong, and they occupied such good positions, that it was almost impossible for their enemies to capture them.

The capital of the Chickasaw was Old Houlka, the Indian name meaning sacred place. It stood not far from present-day Houston.

The Choctaw erected strong, compact, fortified villages, but they also had a kind of "plantation system," with cabin homes spaced a considerable distance from each other, generally about the sound of a gunshot apart. In the center of Choctaw country stood Nanih Waiya, the sacred mound of the Choctaw, near Noxapater. Around this elevation, where legend said life had been created, revolved the life of the tribe.

The Choctaw were the most democratic as well as the most peaceful of the Indians of present-day Mississippi. Their chiefs earned their positions almost entirely through their ability, and they had little authority except as counselors.

Polygamy was permitted by the Choctaw, but the husband or the wife could obtain a divorce whenever either one wished to end the marriage. The children were always given to the mother, and the father had no further control over them.

OTHER INDIAN PRACTICES AND CUSTOMS

Indian babies were given great care. Especially important was the daily rubbing with oil, which helped to keep the mosquitoes away. Children were surprisingly well behaved. For all ages the penalty for quarreling was to be forced to live alone for a certain period of time. This punishment was so feared by young and old alike that the communities lived in surprising peace. However, warfare between rival groups was almost constant.

Indian warfare consisted mostly of ambushes and surprise attacks. Sometimes these surprise attacks were so successful that almost an entire Indian nation would be wiped out. The remnants would then apply to be adopted by a neutral group, and so the defeated group no longer had a separate existence.

The Chickasaw and Choctaw Indians were able to survive.

Agriculture was the great sustainer of Indian life in the region, with the Choctaw the most earnest and skilled farmers. They sometimes even supplied their enemy the Chickasaw with corn, which was the staple crop. Other crops were melons, pumpkins, beans, and sunflowers. Ground was prepared with stone hoes, and seeds were planted in holes drilled by pointed sticks. Children were stationed in small booths in the fields as living scarecrows.

During winter, the men made hunting trips to add to the food supplies, going as far east as the Carolinas and north as Ohio.

Indian winter homes were permanent cabins made of upright posts set in the ground. The chinks were filled with clay, moss, bark, or mud. Pine or cypress bark was so skillfully woven for roofs that they sometimes lasted 20 or even 30 years, never leaking. Only two openings were made —a hole in the roof to let out the smoke, and a door, never more than 3 or 4 feet (about .9 or 1.2 meters) high.

Ornaments and tools were fashioned from almost any hard object such as bone, horns, shells, and teeth. Arrowheads were made from bone and horn almost as frequently as from stone. Many of the Indians were especially skilled in pottery making.

The Indians were very fond of games. One of the most popular was a kind of combination lacrosse and soccer, in which players tossed a ball toward a goal using sticks with woven cups at the end. The Indians were obsessed with gambling. Individuals would bet almost anything they owned—horses, clothing, and other possessions—on the outcome of a game. Large portions of territory were gambled away.

THE "WHITE GODS" RETURN

According to Indian legend, at one time a race of giant white gods enjoyed the easy living in the beautiful area where the Biloxi Indians later made their home. Legend said that these white gods went away to the east, but the legend also foretold that they would come back someday and reclaim their ancestral lands.

There was little surprise one day when the legend seemed to be fulfilled with the appearance of a great, white-winged ship from which came white gods, smaller than the Indians expected but still "god-like" in appearance and even more to be revered in the possessions they carried with them.

Leader of the "gods" was Pierre Lemoyne, Sieur d'Iberville, who anchored his craft off present-day Ship Island. After exploring the coast he decided on Ocean Springs as the first European settlement in the entire southern Mississippi Valley. The year was 1699.

The legend of the white gods probably was created because of earlier European visitors who had passed through parts of the region but who had never stayed to live there.

A mural by William H. Powell, in the Capitol at Washington, depicts the discovery of the Mississippi River by De Soto in 1541.

The first of these white explorers to visit present-day Mississippi was the Spanish conquistador Hernando de Soto and his incredible expedition. They entered Mississippi in 1540 about 8 miles (about 12.8 kilometers) north of present-day Columbus, and most authorities say they were the first Europeans ever to see the great river that gives the state its name. There is a good deal of disagreement as to where this discovery first took place, but de Soto and his weakened forces probably crossed the Mississippi in May, 1541, somewhere near where the US Highway 49 now crosses.

The cruelties of de Soto and his men to the Indians, his capture of hundreds of Indian men and women for slaves, the disturbance and the disease which the Europeans brought probably were the main reasons for the decline and even disappearance of many Indians of the region. De Soto was never to leave the region he had plundered. He died soon after discovering the Mississippi, and at night, his body was slipped into the river secretly, so that the Indians would not know the great leader was dead. This watery grave was probably somewhere near present-day Natchez.

SMALL BEGINNINGS

During the 132 years that followed, many ships passed along the shore; others anchored, and their crews went ashore. There were Spanish adventurers and others who penetrated into the interior, but their visits had little meaning in the history of Mississippi.

In 1629 and 1633, the king of England had included much of present-day Mississippi in granting Carolina to his followers, but this remained only a paper claim.

The kindly Father Jacques Marquette and Louis Jolliet in 1673 made their famous voyage down the Mississippi, reaching a point somewhat below the mouth of the Arkansas River. Even more important was the visit in 1682 of Robert René Cavelier, Sieur de la Salle, who managed to explore the Mississippi River from Illinois to its mouth. With a sweeping ceremony he claimed the entire region drained by the Mississippi River in the name of the king of France.

Other French explorers—Tonti, Hennepin, Cadillac—helped to strengthen the French claim in the vast region.

To make good on the French claim, in 1698 King Louis XIV commissioned d'Iberville to occupy the region which would be known as Louisiana. This was a large order for 200 settlers, but they made their beginning by building Fort Maurepas (now Ocean Springs) in 1699. This tiny fort became the capital of a land extending to Colorado and Montana.

The English, however, had not forgotten their claim, and sent an expedition to seize the lower part of the Mississippi River. About 50 miles (about 80.5 kilometers) from the mouth they met d'Iberville's brother, Jean Baptiste Lemoyne, Sieur de Bienville. Bienville bluffed the English into giving up and turning back. The place where they retreated has been known ever since as English Turn.

With the coming of war between France and England, d'Iberville was ordered to move his capital from the Biloxi area to Mobile, now in Alabama. However, Fort Maurepas remained inhabited. Bienville and d'Iberville also established a number of posts in the interior of present-day Mississippi, among them Fort Rosalie, founded in 1716 on the bluffs of the Mississippi River, the beginning of Natchez.

GREAT SCHEMES

In 1712 the French king gave commercial rights in the Louisiana area to Anthony Crozat. He set up businesses from Illinois to the Gulf Coast, lead mines, mills, and other activities, but the great wilderness was too vast to be conquered by such a comparatively small effort.

The king next turned to a strange figure, John Law, to develop his vast but still unprofitable empire in the Mississippi Valley. Ambitious plans for settlement and development were made. In 1720, three hundred colonists came to settle around Natchez, and about as many went to the Pascagoula area. Other settlers came, but still the region refused to give up the wealth which its French owners hoped to get from it. John Law's ''Mississippi Bubble'' burst; the

Modern Choctaw playing an ancestral game.

people of France had invested so heavily on the hope of getting wealth from the Mississippi area that France almost collapsed when the bubble burst.

MORE DIFFICULTIES

Settlers in Mississippi were almost forgotten by the mother country, and many would have starved without the help of faithful Indian friends. In 1723 the capital was moved to New Orleans.

Bienville, who was able to get along well with the Indians, was replaced by a harsh new governor Perier. Soon Indian troubles increased. In 1729 the Natchez Indians massacred the settlers at Fort Rosalie (now Natchez). The next year, in revenge, a French force nearly wiped out the Natchez. Their leader, the Great Sun, was captured and sent into slavery, the remnants of the group were dispersed, and the Natchez ceased to exist as a group.

Most of the success the French had in their early settlements came from trade with the Indians, principally for the furs the Indians gathered in such great quantities. The French wanted to extend this trade farther north, but the Chickasaw Indians had allied themselves with the British. British colonies on the East Coast had grown strong, and a constantly increasing number of British traders were pushing into the interior.

The French set out to conquer the Chickasaw, but with British help the Chickasaw defeated every French effort to unite the Gulf colonies with the French colonies in Illinois and Indiana. The first of these French defeats came in 1730.

29

Chickasaw attacks against the French settlements, even as far south as the Gulf, continued, until Bienville, who had returned as governor, decided to wipe the Chickasaw from the map. Instead, he suffered a series of disasters. In 1736 Bienville attacked the Chickasaw town of Aekia on the Pontotoc Ridge, where the Indians won a great victory. In some ways this was one of the decisive battles of history. French fortunes in North America declined from this point on until the French were driven from the continent.

The clash between France and Britain for control of the continent came to a head in the French and Indian War. When in 1762 the French saw they soon would have to give up, they turned over control of all of the Mississippi Valley west of the river as well as New Orleans to Spain. In 1763 the French and Indian War ended and, by the Treaty of Paris, France was forced to turn over the rest of her American colonies to England. This included all land east of the Mississippi River from its headwaters, including the Gulf Coast. The Spanish kept control of New Orleans, but ceded Florida to Great Britain after the British took possession of Pensacola and St. Augustine; the English king established the provinces of East Florida and West Florida.

BRITISH CONTROL, THEN REVOLUTION

Most of present-day Mississippi was in British hands after 1763. It was included in British West Florida. British army veterans were given land grants in the Natchez region, and many settlers came in under British encouragement. Fort Rosalie was reconstructed with the new name of Panmure, later Natchez. In many ways the colony of Natchez deserved to be considered a fourteenth British colony.

However, when the Revolutionary War broke out, the colonists of British West Florida (including the Natchez district) were not interested in revolting against the British. Actually, they were not in a position to do so if they had wished. Many Tories (those who remained loyal to Britain) fled to Natchez from the eastern colonies, bringing with them as much of their wealth as they could.

30

The American colonies sent a representative, James Willing, to Natchez. Willing persuaded the people to remain neutral, but because he was personally dishonest he had no success in making the Natchez settlers turn toward the other colonies.

The Revolutionary forces received a good deal of help from Spain. Britain had taken over the Gulf region, but Spanish forces under Governor Don Bernardo de Galvez reconquered the Biloxi area in 1779. Spanish troops moved up the Mississippi in 1779 and seized Natchez. By 1781, British West Florida was in the hands of the Spanish.

AN AMERICAN TERRITORY

The treaty of peace in 1783 gave the new United States all of British territory in present-day Mississippi as far south as the 31st parallel, the line which now marks the southern boundary of Mississippi with Louisiana. Spain, however, refused to recognize this, and tried to keep control of the region as far north as the 32nd parallel, a line almost 40 miles (about 64 kilometers) north of Natchez.

Spain rapidly expanded and strengthened the Natchez region, and in 1790 received a grant from the Indians to build an outpost as far north as present-day Vicksburg, which was called Fort Nogalles.

Nevertheless, in the Treaty of Madrid in 1795, the Spanish government at last agreed to recognize the boundary at the 31st parallel, and the United States was also given the right to use the Mississippi River freely throughout its whole length. The American representative, Andrew Ellicott, reached Natchez in 1797 and raised the American flag unofficially, but the Spanish refused to leave until March 30, 1798. Then for the first time the American flag went up officially over Natchez.

The Territory of Mississippi (also including most of present-day Alabama) was established by an act of Congress, April 7, 1798. Major Isaac Guion was in command until the first governor, Winthrop Sargent, arrived in Natchez, capital of the territory.

A full oyster dredge enters the Biloxi harbor.

Yesterday and Today

AMERICA STRUGGLES FOR CONTROL

In 1803 the territory that Spain had turned over to France was bought by the United States in what is known as the Louisiana Purchase. However, Spain remained in control of Florida. This territory included an extension of the present-day Florida panhandle which reached clear to the Mississippi at Baton Rouge, Louisiana.

The English, French, and American settlers of the Natchez region had not yet become "Americanized," but they were held together by a general feeling of hatred for Spain. When Aaron Burr, formerly Vice-President of the United States, was arrested for treason in 1807, some of the people of Mississippi were in sympathy with him. They thought he was planning to set up a new American state in Spanish-held territory.

Guerrilla warfare between American settlers and Spanish officials began and continued for several years. Finally, in 1810, American settlers in Spanish West Florida revolted and declared themselves the Republic of West Florida. As soon as possible, the Federal government added this region, extending nearly to present Mobile, Alabama, to the United States, calling it the Territory of Orleans.

Meanwhile, the British had never been reconciled to giving up the vast territories of the eastern Mississippi Valley. All over this region they encouraged the Indians to attack the American settlers. The powerful Chief Tecumseh visited most of the Indians in this region, urging them to join him in a move to throw out all the settlers of the Mississippi Valley region.

This move might have succeeded if Pushmataha, a Choctaw chief who was friendly to the Americans, had not refused to cooperate with Tecumseh. The British and Americans went to war once more in the War of 1812, and the British encouraged their Indian allies to join. In the Gulf region the Creek nation went on the warpath. Only the appearance of Andrew Jackson with volunteers from Tennessee, who joined the Mississippians, defeated the Creek warriors. In the final naval battle of the war, a small fleet of American warships

Zachary Taylor's plantation, Cypress Grove near Rodney, was typical of the great plantations. Painting by H. Lewis.

under Lieutenant Thomas Catesby Jones was overwhelmed by a much larger British fleet near Bay St. Louis in 1814. The British then occupied Ship Island, from which to attack New Orleans.

However, popular Andrew Jackson was able to prepare New Orleans for the British attack. One of his moves in this connection was to fortify the mouth of the Pearl River. In the period just before the war and during the four years of war, a wave of American settlers (known as the Great Migration) had flooded into Mississippi, most of them floating down the Ohio and Mississippi rivers on keelboats and flatboats. From these and the early settlers, Jackson was able to assemble a considerable force of defenders from Mississippi, to add to his forces from other regions. Nearly every male citizen of Natchez helped Jackson win the Battle of New Orleans.

STATEHOOD

During the period from 1800 onward, Mississippi experienced all the excitement, confusion, and disorganization of a frontier territory. Pirates, such as the notorious Jean Lafitte and Pierre Rameau

King of Honey Island, were said to be working in friendly cooperation with residents and officials all along the coast. Settlement was increasing rapidly, and the settlers, as in most frontiers, were reluctant to submit to law and order. They disagreed violently with the first territorial governor, Winthrop Sargent, who was appointed in Washington and not elected by the people.

Because so many governments had ruled in the region, there was additional confusion. Land grants had been issued by France, Spain, England, by the United States, by the Republic of West Florida, and even by Georgia, which at one time claimed large areas. The resulting complications of land titles and other legal rights were so difficult to unravel that sometimes the population appeared to be made up mostly of lawyers.

As early as 1811, Mississippi's territorial delegate to Congress had been attempting to get an enabling act passed so that Mississippi could become a state. Finally, following the census taken in 1816, Congress agreed to permit the region to organize for statehood; the enabling act was passed on March 1, 1817. The following summer a constitution, written mostly by George Poindexter, was adopted by the constitutional convention meeting in Washington, near Natchez, July 7 to August 15. On December 10, 1817, the new state of Mississippi was born, with the last territorial governor, David Holmes, the first elected state governor. The territorial capital had been moved from Natchez to Washington in 1808, but the constitution of 1817 designated Natchez to be the state capital. Natchez remained the capital until the capital was moved to Columbia, then, after only three months, to its location at Jackson in 1821. The city had been created especially as the capital, and the first session of the legislature there named the town in honor of Andrew Jackson.

KING COTTON'S KINGDOM

During the years after 1800 nothing in the state's history was more spectacular than the rise of cotton as the principal product of Mississippi. The invention of Whitney's cotton gin in 1797 and machine methods of weaving cloth had set the stage for rapidly expanded use of cotton, and Mississippi's rich lands were ideal for growing cotton. Men of wealth and position from other states, especially of the South but also from abroad, moved in, bought huge plantations at low prices and rapidly set up vast cotton-growing operations, using thousands of slaves.

At first the type of cotton which was grown was not very choice. Then in 1806 better quality cotton seed was brought in from Mexico. The new seed, named Petit Gulf in honor of the plantation where it was first used, became widespread, and was most successful.

As planters became more wealthy, they came to dominate the state government; they built imposing plantation houses and created an aristocracy of a type never seen before or since in America.

THE TRAIL OF TEARS

The demand for more cotton land and the rapid increase of settlers placed great pressure on the Indians. By this time the Choctaw and the Chickasaw had improved their conditions until they were ranked as two of the five important Indian groups of the United States. Their leaders and wealthy individuals owned farms, built comfortable houses, and some owned black slaves.

Settlers looked with envy on this Indian wealth and fine land. Pressure increased for the Indians to sell their land to the government and move to Oklahoma, known as Indian Territory. By treaties made in 1801, 1805, and 1820, the Indians already had given up all of the state except the east-central and north portions.

After long and bitter argument, the Choctaw finally agreed to sign the Treaty of Dancing Rabbit, giving up their land for new land in Oklahoma, along with certain government payments. Leflore persuaded the government to agree to let any Indian families stay if they wished, and to give them each 100 acres (about 40 hectares) of land, protected by the United States. Three thousand Choctaw warriors refused to go to Oklahoma, but it took the government 100 years to begin to keep the promise to help them.

36

The sturdy Chickasaw were the last to surrender. They held out until 1832, when at last they felt they must give in, and they signed the Treaty of Pontotoc, agreeing to leave their ancestral land.

During the 1830s, there were scenes of the deepest despair in Mississippi as the Indians left their homes to embark on the long hard "Trail of Tears" across the country to far-off Oklahoma.

GROWTH AND DEVELOPEMENT

By 1832 the people of Mississippi were ready for a new state constitution. The newer settlers had ideas of wider rule by the people, and these were included in the new Mississippi Constitution adopted in that year. This constitution has been called the most democratic of any of the states at the time. It even provided for the election of judges.

Another advance was made in 1839 when the government of Mississippi became the first in the English speaking world to recognize by law the property rights of women.

During this period many of the river towns were also "wide open." At Vicksburg the river gamblers congregated and bragged that they controlled the town. Hardly a night passed without a number of knifings, shootings, or at the least beatings. However, when a respected local doctor was shot, the citizens lynched several gamblers, gained the upper hand, and established law and order.

Natchez also had its "Under-the-Hill" area, known for years for its wickedness.

Possibly even more dangerous for society was the attitude of some men of the leading families, who seemed to have a contempt for their own welfare and of others. Although illegal, duels were fought, often for the slightest reason.

Lawlessness lessened, of course, as settlement and social growth continued until, according to figures released by the FBI, in 1966, Mississippi had the second lowest crime rate of the fifty states.

The rapid sweep of settlement is illustrated by the Federal census figures of Mississippi population: 1820—75,448; 1830—136,621;

1840—375,651; 1850—606,526; and 1860—791,305. Agriculture, education, transportation, mining, and manufacturing all played their parts.

PRELUDE TO TRAGEDY

In the years before 1861 nothing was so important in Mississippi as the plantation system, which depended completely on cotton and on the use of ever-increasing numbers of slaves to grow it. Mississippi leaders encouraged every opportunity to expand the slave system.

Such leading figures of the state as Jefferson Davis, John A. Quitman, Henry S. Foote, and Robert J. Walker encouraged Texas independence in every way possible. They and many others promoted war with Mexico to provide help for Texas and to lay the basis for taking over other Mexican territory.

Much of the work of Mississippi leaders was directed toward all activities that would bring new slave states into the Union to balance the free states coming in. Mississippi leaders were among the most effective workers in this regard.

Before war came, however, there was a good deal of sentiment against any break with the Union. Many of the older families of wealth and large numbers of poorer people who had no stake in the slave system were strongly opposed to any split in the United States. Nevertheless, as the quarrel between North and South became more bitter, the policy of the state toward slavery became even more firm, supported by vast numbers of the middle class.

WAR COMES!

The final break came in Mississippi at Jackson at 10:00 A.M., January 9, 1861, when the state was the second to secede from the Union. War enthusiasm was heightened when Mississippian Jefferson Davis became the President of the Confederate States. Another Mississippi man, Stephen D. Lee of Columbus, took part in the opening of the

On May 19, 1863, the United States Infantry attacked part of the Vicksburg defenses called "Stockade Redan." From an army poster painted by H. Charles McBarron.

war as one of the two Confederate officers sent to demand Fort Sumter to surrender. During the first year of war, there was little actual fighting on Mississippi soil, with the exception of the occupation by Federal forces of Ship Island on the Gulf Coast. They used this position to help blockade the Confederate coast. However, the state poured its treasures into the war, and troops from Mississippi took part in the early battles elsewhere. There were five regiments from the state at the first Battle of Manassas.

Mississippi first felt the direct effect of war during the Battle of Shiloh in April, 1862, as the battle raged back and forth across the Mississippi and Tennessee boundary.

The Union plan was to cut the South in two by capturing and controlling the Mississippi. Union naval forces were moving up the river from New Orleans and down the river from Illinois. The strongest Confederate point on the river was Vicksburg. As long as Confederate forces held Vicksburg, Union gunboats could not have free use of the Mississippi. The Battle of Shiloh was part of the Union move to sweep down from the north and capture this important point.

After Shiloh, Union General Halleck brought 100,000 troops against Corinth, and northern Mississippi was a battleground for the rest of the year as fighting raged at Iuka, Bonneville, Chickasaw Bayou, Tallahatchie Bridge, Coffeeville, and Holly Springs.

Union General Ulysses S. Grant made Holly Springs his storage center for the coming two-sided attack on Vicksburg. However, Confederate General Earl Van Dorn mounted a fierce surprise attack on Holly Springs, destroyed over $4,000,000 worth of Grant's supplies, and recaptured the town. This great success delayed the capture of Vicksburg for a year and kept vast numbers of Union troops and equipment from use in other battlefields.

THE SOUTH LOSES ITS "GIBRALTAR"

The next attempt to take Vicksburg began in January, 1863. By April 30, 1863, Grant's army had crossed the Mississippi at Bruinsburg. Then followed the series of battles which prevented the Confederate armies of Pemberton and Johnston from joining forces. In 17 days Grant marched 130 miles (about 209 kilometers) and split Confederate forces which would have outnumbered him if combined, and he arrived at the back door of Vicksburg.

After Grant tried two assaults on Vicksburg and lost 4,000 men, he then decided to lay siege to the city. Admiral Porter's Western Flotilla of ironclads and gunboats managed to slip into position by night and now—mounting over 300 guns and carrying 5,500 men— occupied the river. Big guns and more troops arrived to ring the city; from then on nothing, or no one, could get in to help Vicksburg.

All during May and June the siege continued. The Union artillery and the river mortars kept up an almost ceaseless shelling of the city, forcing the civilian population to dig caves in the hillsides for protection. It seemed that the only time the screaming of the shells stopped was when the Union gunners stopped to eat.

For 47 days Vicksburg was bombarded and starved, with Union encirclement growing steadily closer and stronger and the ability of the city to fight back growing desperately weaker daily. Ammunition was becoming low, and the people were starving. Knowing that they could not survive much longer, General Pemberton arranged with Grant to surrender Vicksburg, "The Gibraltar of the Confederacy," and its army of 29,500 on July 4, 1863.

As the Confederate skeletons marched out in rags to stack their rifles, cartridge boxes, and flags before the massed Union army, there was only a respectful hush. The Union forces remembered the heroism of the defenders and that the North also had lost a terrible number—16,000—in that battle.

From that time on the Confederacy was cut off from all help west of the Mississippi River, and Federal forces could use the waterway to carry vast amounts of supplies for their attacks in the South.

DESPERATE TIMES

Union General William Tecumseh Sherman laid siege to Jackson on July 11, and the city was captured July 17. The capital city was burned, and Sherman was able to report to Grant, "We have made fine progress today in the work of destruction. Jackson will no longer be a point of danger."

Natchez was also bombarded in July and was occupied by Federal forces.

In 1864 bitter fighting continued along the Mississippi River area between Vicksburg and Natchez, at Meridian, Okolona, Brice's Crossroads, Tupelo, and Egypt.

Concerning Meridian, Sherman wrote: "For five days 10,000 men worked hard with a will in that work of destruction with axes, crowbars, sledges, clawbars, and fire, and I have no hesitation in pronouncing the work well done. Meridian . . . no longer exists."

At the Battle of Brice's Crossroads Confederate General Nathan Bedford Forrest routed a much larger Union force and captured large quantities of wagons and supplies.

He was not so successful at the Battle of Tupelo on July 14, 1864, one of the bloodiest ever fought in Mississippi. In spite of their victory, the Union troops under General A.J. Smith withdrew unexpectedly, abandoning two hundred fifty severely wounded men. Historian Robert S. Henry wrote, "It was a strange spectacle, an army which had just won a pitched battle drawing back from an enemy of half its own size which it had just beaten."

The Battle of Tupelo was the last major battle in Mississippi. During early 1865, there were raids and minor engagements at Iuka, Corinth, Friar's Point, Fort Adams, Rodney, and Port Gibson. On May 4, 1865, following Lee's surrender at Appomattox, General Taylor surrendered the Confederate forces in Mississippi.

"WAR IS HELL"

More than 80,000 men from Mississippi served in the Confederate forces. This total was greater than the entire number of men of fighting age in Mississippi as listed in the 1860 census. Of those who served, a total of 60,000 died. This is undoubtedly the highest percentage of deaths of any state during the war.

Much of the state had been burned or otherwise destroyed. The wealth of generations had vanished. The suffering during the war is illustrated by such examples as the sixty-one separate raids endured by Holly Springs. The once thriving capital of the state came to be known as Chimneyville, since throughout most of the town only its gaunt chimneys remained.

Oxford was described by travelers as "the most utterly demolished town ever seen."

As he considered his devastating march across the state, General Sherman said, "The wholesale destruction is terrible to contemplate." He was approaching Pearl River near Jackson when Sherman made the most often-quoted of his remarks, "War is hell."

The confusion of the times is illustrated in another way by the rapid shifting of the capital due to the war—hurriedly moved from Jackson to Enterprise, then to Meridian, returned for a time to Jackson, again to Meridian, then Columbus, after which it was at Macon, and at last back to Jackson.

POCKETS OF RESISTANCE

There were some in Mississippi who opposed the Confederacy and that some opposition continued throughout the war. Stone County is said never to have been occupied by a slaveholder.

In Jones County, some of the people called their area "The Free State of Jones." They formed a guerrilla band of about one hundred twenty-five men under the leadership of Newt Knight. Guerrilla warfare continued in the region during the entire war, and Knight and his men hid out in the Leaf River swamps around Ellisville, where most of them managed to escape capture.

One of the most bitter opponents of secession was the great Choctaw Chief Greenwood Leflore. All during the war, in defiance of the Confederates, the American flag flew over Malmaison, the Leflore mansion. Confederate sympathizers once tried to kill Leflore and an attempt was made to burn Malmaison, but Leflore remained loyal to the Union. After his death on August 21, 1865, he was buried wrapped in the American flag.

AWFUL AFTERMATH

After the war came the bitter period known as Reconstruction. Although civil officers were advised they were not included in the capitulation of the military, almost immediately Governor Charles Clark was arrested in his office and was a prisoner for a few weeks at Fort Pulaski until released on parole. President Andrew Johnson appointed Judge William L. Sharkey as provisional governor. A constitutional convention amended the state constitution to abolish slavery, and General Benjamin G. Humphreys was elected governor. However, when the Mississippi legislature refused to approve the 13th and 14th amendments to the United States Constitution, the state was put under military law, and Governor Humphreys was forcibly ejected from his office by Lieutenant Colonel Adelbert Ames, who became the military governor.

By 1869 anyone who had served under the Confederacy was forbidden to hold office, and state offices were filled by blacks, carpetbaggers (those who had hurried down from the North to take advantage of the situation), and scalawags (people of the South who took advantage of their own people).

In 1870 Mississippi was readmitted to the Union under the control of a Reconstruction governor and legislature. Extravagant and corrupt administrations in state and local offices increased the distress left after the war and made recovery almost impossible. The people found their hardships almost unbearable, and by the election of 1875, both sides had turned to violence and terrorism.

For the years between 1871 and 1875 the state had been torn by riots, in six out of its present eighty-two counties, with the race riot at Clinton in September, 1875 one of the worst of the whole period of Reconstruction. The following day rumors that fourteen hundred blacks had started a march on Vicksburg led to another of the worst riots during Reconstruction. However, it ended carpetbag rule in that city.

After the bitter campaign of 1875, a coalition of Democrats and Whigs began to restore order to the state government. When Reconstruction Governor Adelbert Ames was impeached and resigned from office, John M. Stone became governor in 1876 and led Mississippi from Reconstruction control.

One of Mississippi's congressmen, Lucius Quintus Cincinnatus Lamar, is credited with an act which helped to reconcile the North and South. He made a moving and now famous speech in Congress in praise of the Northern leader Charles Sumner, who had died, and this did much to heal the sectional wounds.

"Let us hope," he said, "that future generations, when they

remember the deeds of heroism and devotion done on both sides, will speak not of Northern prowess and Southern courage, but of the heroism, fortitude and courage of Americans in a war of ideas, a war in which each section signalized its consecration to the principles, as each understood them, of American liberty and of the Constitution received from their fathers."

However, the disasters of the war and the ten years of suffering during the Reconstruction period following it have left effects and scars from which the state has not recovered even yet. Among other things, Mississippi steadfastly refused to ratify the 13th amendment to the United States Constitution, which freed the slaves.

A MODERN STATE

In addition to man-made troubles, other calamities hit Mississippi during this period. Among the worst of these were the plagues of disease, such as the yellow fever epidemic of 1878, in which two thousand people died at Holly Springs alone.

One of the most forward-looking works of the legislature was an act of 1882 "to encourage the establishment of factories in this state and to exempt them from taxation."

Attention of the sports world turned to Hattiesburg in 1889 when the country's last bare-knuckle championship boxing meet was held there—between John L. Sullivan and Jack Kilrain. In spite of the efforts of the governor and the militia, the illegal bout got under way and went for seventy-five rounds before Kilrain's seconds threw in the towel.

The present constitution of Mississippi was approved in 1890.

Over the years the influence of the small farmer had increased, and by 1904 their leader, James K. Vardaman, known as the "Great White Chief," had been elected governor. The long control of the state by the planter class had ended.

One of the gravest disturbances came in 1909 when the boll weevil began to threaten the cotton crop. In the long run there was some benefit in this disaster, because it compelled farmers of the state to turn to other kinds of profitable crops, such as oats, soybeans, and corn.

Mississippi became the nation's "Winter White House" in the winter of 1913-14, when Woodrow Wilson and his family spent part of the winter at Pass Christian in the house owned by Mrs. J. A. Ayers. In the warming sun of the coast, the President improved greatly from an attack of influenza. In one incident the President discovered a fire in a neighboring house and helped put it out. More important was a secret conference of the President on board the scout cruiser *Chester* off Gulfport, in which the Chief Executive conferred with experts on the crisis with Mexico.

To celebrate the one hundred years of Mississippi's statehood, Gulfport prepared a great centennial exposition for 1917. The exposition grounds were to provide a permanent exhibit of Mississippi commerce. Before the show opened the United States entered World War I, and the exposition was never held.

During the war, about 66,000 men and women from Mississippi were members of the armed services, and 2,303 suffered casualties, of whom 904 died. Camp Shelby was one of the country's most important training centers, with as many as 60,000 servicemen stationed there at one time.

Because of low land values forced by low cotton prices, the depletion of timber resources, and other reasons, Mississippi was in a depressed state even before the great depression of the 1930s. The state budget could not be balanced for several years. However, during the period of 1925-35 there was a slow movement toward manufacturing, although agriculture and forestry continued to be the keystones of the state's business life.

The Mississippi River flood of 1927 was the worst ever experienced in the lower reaches of the river. In the emergency, the bluffs and hills of Vicksburg provided a refuge for thousands of flood victims. After the flood, Congressman William Whittington of Washington County introduced the bill which at last placed flood control under the Federal government. Before this time, efforts to curb floods had been carried on piecemeal by states and other local governments.

Among the many safeguards and improvements made was the cutting of the canal which shortened the Mississippi at Natchez.

One of the most disastrous tornadoes in the country killed 201 at Tupelo in 1936.

Also that year, Governor Hugh White's program to Balance Agriculture With Industry (BAWI) was adopted. This program was widely imitated in other states and was a pioneering effort on the part of united political and business leadership of the state to secure progress for Mississippi.

During World War II 202,560 Mississippians were in service, and 4,187 died. In the Korean War in 1950-51, more Mississippi men won the Congressional Medal than men of any other state. These were Mack A. Jordan, Jack G. Hanson, John A. Pittman, Hubert L. Lee, and John J. Tominac.

The war and postwar years were marked by expansion and growth in almost every part of the state's economy.

On May 21, 1966, Mississippi became the last state in the country to abandon prohibition.

In 1967 the state truly entered the space age with the completion of the $350 million NASA static test center in Hancock County, now called the National Space Technology Laboratories.

As the nation celebrated its Bicentennial in 1976, Mississippi joined with a statewide program of events. For the nation's third century, Mississippi could look forward to a stable but growing economy, with its many people able to anticipate generally increased standards of living and unparalleled personal freedom.

THE PEOPLE OF MISSISSIPPI

The first European settlers in what is now Mississippi were not very desirable; in fact, they have been called the "scum of France." To rid itself of them, France sent convicts, adventurers, and such whether they wished to come or not. At last, however, the government realized its mistake and began to encourage a better class of settlers. They also recruited a group of fine young ladies to emigrate to America to find husbands, and each was given a marriage outfit. Because they brought this with them in a wooden chest, or *casquette*, they were called the "Casket Girls."

Since the first settlers came, people of almost every nationality settled in Mississippi, such as Biloxi's people of Polish, Austrian, Czech, and Yugoslav backgrounds. Today, Mississippi has the smallest number of people of foreign birth of any state.

Among the interesting groups are the Acadians of Deslisle, and others of the so-called Creole strain, a term which is applied to native-born Americans of French and Spanish parentage or ancestry.

Another interesting group has been the hill people, at one time isolated and clannish and often not enjoying modern advantages. They lived a picturesque and self-sufficient life, enjoying occasional drives to town in the wagon, the social life of the church, ballads, tournaments, and other old-time recreation. Now, however, such life is rapidly vanishing.

Today, as it has been since the time of English control, most of the white population of Mississippi is of Anglo-Saxon background.

The first blacks came to Mississippi almost with the start of the French settlement. The black population skyrocketed with the sad and seemingly endless importation of slaves to man the cotton plantations. With freedom after the Civil War, the bright prospects of mutual respect and rights among the races were expected by many, but they quickly dimmed, as blacks were given positions in the Reconstruction government that they were not equipped to fill, while the majority were denied the education and labor that might have permitted a gradual improvement in their situation. By far the largest numbers, along with almost equally large numbers of whites, became involved in the tenant-credit system, which developed of necessity at the end of the Civil War. The freed slaves and the landless whites had nowhere to go, and the landowners had no cash with which to pay for labor. Under the tenant-credit system, the landowner agreed to house, clothe, and feed the tenant family on credit until the crops were harvested in return for their labor; they were then paid whatever was due them after their expenses were deducted. This system at its worst led on the one hand to exploitation by an unscrupulous landowner whose tenants rarely, if ever, managed to get out of debt to the owner, or, on the other hand, to the owner receiving inefficient labor about six months of the year. The dual evils of the system retarded agricultural and economic development in the rural South for a number of years.

The black population of Mississippi was listed as 815,770 in the 1970 census.

In 1976 it was estimated that nearly three hundred thousand black citizens were registered to vote. As early as 1967, twenty-four blacks were elected to office in Mississippi, one to the legislature. By 1976, eighty-six blacks had been elected to office, four in the legislature.

Mississippi's memorial to pioneer hero Sam Dale.

Truck farmers grow a variety of products.

Natural Treasures

GROWING THINGS

Nearly 60 percent of Mississippi is still classified as forest land. This is an area about equal in size to the combined areas of Vermont, New Hampshire, and Massachusetts.

Mississippi forests are highly productive, favored with ample rainfall and a long growing season. They can produce more than a cord of wood per acre per year on the average. Improved planning and management is making this productivity increase year by year.

At present, Mississippi is growing more softwood timber each year than is being used, but interest in reforestation has also hit an all-time high. Tree planting was started in the state in earnest in the 1930s; today some fifty to sixty million tree seedlings are set out yearly. The state is first in the nation in the number of certified tree farms, and as less land is being planted in crops, acreage devoted to trees is being increased. At the same time, approximately half of the state's original forest area is still producing timber.

Pine, oak, and gum are the principal trees of the state, including loblolly pine, shortleaf pine, longleaf pine, slash pine, white oak, water oak, red oak; others are sweet gum, black gum, hickory, yellow poplar, pecan, beech, ash, cottonwood, willow, and cypress.

The greatest problem is in the field of the hardwood, where use still exceeds new growth, but efforts are being made constantly to increase productivity.

Mississippi is the only state where the state flower is the blossom of the state tree. When the huge, waxy, white blossom of the magnolia bursts open in the spring, few would question that Mississippi's state flower is magnificent. It was chosen by a vote of the school children in 1900. The magnolia tree itself, with its heavy, dark green, glistening foliage and its lovely shapeliness also must rank among the most outstanding arboreal symbols of the states.

The extensive plant life, including abundant varieties of wildflowers, ranges in variety from the mountain laurel of the uplands to the striking Spanish bayonet in the lower regions.

LIVING CREATURES

The forests and prairies of Mississippi once teemed with animals. Countless buffalo, wildcat, cougar, bear, and wolf made their way over the forest paths or across the open regions. The buffalo, the bear, the beaver, and the otter were exterminated for food and furs. The beaver, however, have reappeared in small numbers.

Deer also at one time were almost gone, but thanks to the efforts of conservationists and the Fish and Game Commission, hunters again enjoy a deer season.

On the state's hunting areas are found not only white tail deer, but also squirrels, bob-white quail, and the magnificent wild turkey, along with other game birds and fur-bearers. Dove hunters enjoy a split season, in September and in the winter. Public waterfowl management areas are also found on some of the reservoirs and river areas where duck and other waterfowl gather. Wild ducks are hunted along the great Mississippi River flyway during the short season.

Song birds of Mississippi include the cheerful and tuneful state bird, the mockingbird, cardinal, thrashers (thrushes), pine warbler, Bachman's sparrow, brown-headed nuthatch, red-cockaded woodpecker, and many others. Rumors still persist that the prized ivorybilled woodpecker can still be seen, although it has been thought extinct for some time. Smaller birds include the prothonotary and hooded warblers, the rare swainson's warbler and indigo bunting. Among the delta birds are the dickcissel, bronzed grackle, and the surprisingly colorful painted bunting.

No very large nesting colonies of water and shore birds are found in Mississippi, but the nesting areas in nearby states assure that many water birds are seen. Brown pelican, terns, as many as thirty-five species of sandpipers, gulls, and plovers are often seen. The great blue heron, poules d'eau, snowy and American egret, and the peculiar anhinga or water turkey are among the more striking members of the Mississippi bird family.

An interesting water creature is the alligator, once extremely common, then almost wiped out, and now, with protection, making a comeback.

52

In the opinion of fishermen, the most important freshwater fish of the state probably would be the black and striped bass along with the buffalo fish, the various catfish, bream, and perch. Red fish, sheepshead, drum, croaker, flounder, and mullet also delight many a fisherman.

Deep sea fish of almost every variety include the spectacular tarpon, speckled trout, mackerel, crevalle, cobia, and many others.

Shrimp, oysters, and other seafoods are abundant.

MINERALS

Perhaps the most important of the many minerals found in Mississippi are oil and natural gas, in over 225 fields. The oil and gas reserves of the state are very extensive.

The state's 51 piercement-type salt domes, analyzed at 99.4 percent pure, are of particular interest in the manufacture of chlorine, bleaches, chlorates, soda ash, and caustic soda. Millions of tons of lignite are present in north Mississippi, and new uses are being found for it constantly.

Other minerals include a wealth of useful clays, marl, cement rock, silica, limestone, sandstone, bentonite, fullers earth, phosphorous, bauxite, and high alumina clays, tripoli, asphaltic rock, glauconite, heavy mineral sands, and ochre.

Possibly the most valuable minerals of all are the productive soil and the plentiful fresh water. Some of the world's richest soil is found in the Mississippi Delta region, and water resources both above ground and in underwater supplies are considered abundant. Just one source—the mighty Mississippi River—has a daily flow of from 300 to 500 billions of gallons (about 1.1 to 1.9 million kiloliters) as it passes the shores of the state.

People Use their Treasures

AGRICULTURE

When the Spaniards took control of Mississippi, they offered to buy all the tobacco that could be grown, and tobacco became the chief crop of the area. When Spain could no longer make good on its promise to buy, many tobacco planters of Misissippi were ruined.

Next the growers turned to indigo, a rapidly growing plant from which blue colors were made. The 3-foot-tall (.91 meters) stalks were cut, tied in bundles, and left to ferment in vats, while the coloring material settled to the bottom. The odor of this process was almost unbearable, but indigo was grown with a good deal of success until advancements in growing and in processing cotton made cotton a profitable crop.

For many generations cotton was king, until the boll weevil forced Mississippi farmers to turn to other crops, and cotton lost its importance. Growing crop after crop of cotton on the same land ruined the soil. As early as the 1850s a scientist wrote: "Even the present generation is rife with complaints about the exhaustion of the soils—in a region which thirty years ago, had but just received the first scratch of the plowshare. In some parts of the state the deserted homesteads and fields . . . might well remind the traveler of the descriptions given of . . . Europe after the Thirty Years' War."

Without protection, the soils also washed away, leaving great desolate gullies. Only in more recent times have farmers learned to add fertilizers to the soil, rotate their crops, and keep the soil from washing away, but much still needs to be done to protect the land and bring it back to its former usefulness.

Today cotton is still very important, and most of the work is done by machinery. Mississippi was a leader in cotton mechanization. Coahoma County produced the first cotton crop in the world in which machinery was used in all phases of the work. The cotton pickers with their picturesque long bags dragging behind them are seen in only a few small fields. Giant picking machines now straddle the rows, dumping the puffy, gleaming white cotton bolls into huge

*After cotton
is picked
and loaded,
it is ready
for processing.*

wire-sided wagons that take them to the gins, from which they go to processing and bailing.

Since 1917, the world's largest inland long staple cotton market has been located at Greenwood, center of the world's greatest long staple region. Other communities of the state also are important in cotton marketing.

Cotton by-products have a growing importance, including cotton-seed oil and a livestock feed made from the seed pulp. Mississippi pioneered in the use of cottonseed oil, which was processed for the first time at Natchez in 1834. Many of the best types of cotton have been developed in the state, and research for new uses goes on constantly. One of the most interesting of these was an experimental road of 1935 paved with cotton mesh laid in asphalt.

Some of the country's largest cotton plantations may still be found in Mississippi, including the 38,000 acre (about 15,000 hectares) Delta and Pine Land Company plantation.

About 1,700,000 acres (about 690,000 hectares) of the state are still devoted to cotton production. This compares with about 2,500,000 (about 1,000,000 hectares) used for soybeans and about 140,000 (about 56,000 hectares) for corn. Other important crops include oats, wheat, and vegetables. The total value of crops in Mississippi is about $821,644,000.

Livestock values add about $800,000,000 to the farm income of Mississippi, making the total income from farms about $1,500,000,000 annually.

Of these totals, cattle brought in $259,466,000, dairy products $70,921,000, and poultry $315,357,000.

MONEY DOES GROW ON TREES

Forest products have traditionally earned a large part of the state's income, and more than two billion dollars a year comes to Mississippi from its forests.

Since the first lumber mill was established in the state at Natchez in 1809, the number of lumber processors has grown until more than 80,000 Mississippians hold jobs in forest-based industry, with an annual payroll of over $400,000,000.

The products known as naval stores—turpentine, rosins, and tars extracted from pine trees—have long been valued in Mississippi. Increasing numbers of trees are tapped each year, and the odor of the oil gives a strong clean smell to the producing regions. In cut-over areas, stumps are pulled or blasted out of the ground. Along with knots and other former waste material, these can be ground up and the naval stores extracted from otherwise useless wood.

Orchards are another source of the "money that grows on trees" in Mississippi. Pecans are the most important orchard product, bringing close to $5,000,000 yearly income to the state. Peach production accounts for about $1,000,000 annual income.

One of the more exotic orchard crops is the tung nut, an Oriental tree. Looking for something to grow in cut-over lands, Mississippi growers brought in this unusual tree. Before the tung industry in Mississippi was nearly destroyed in 1969 by Hurricane Camille, it brought in several million dollars a year.

Picayune was the center of the prosperous tung-growing region. In the spring the white waxy tung blossoms covered the countryside over wide areas, making Mississippi look more like a part of the Orient than the South.

The tung nuts were dried, husked, ground into meal, heated, and pressed to squeeze out the oil, which is used by paint and varnish manufacturers. Husks and residue are used for fertilizers. The state's large processors of tung-nut products were also hard hit by the loss of the trees.

Even Spanish moss—which hangs on trees but derives its life from the air—is collected and used commercially in certain kinds of upholstery and stuffing products.

MANUFACTURING AND MINING

Manufacturing had a slow start in Mississippi because there were few waterfalls or swiftly moving streams, and these were necessary to provide power for industry in the days before steam and electric power plants. The long endeavor to bring manufacturing to the state finally paid off when in 1965 Mississippi joined the ranks of states where manufacturing employed more workers than agriculture, and the value of the product became greater than that of the farms.

Recent figures on value of manufacturing in Mississippi (1973) showed the state producing goods worth more than $3,000,000,000.

Quite naturally, the manufacturing industry is strongest in products based on Mississippi fields and forests, including the four leading categories of manufactured products: food and kindred products ($266,276,400); pulp, paper and paper products ($187,020,000); apparel and related products ($308,120,800); and lumber and wood products ($334,509,000).

A $212,000,000 pulpwood and sawmill plant was established in 1975 at New Augusta by Finnish-based Leaf River Products.

Other important types of manufacturing are chemicals and allied products ($251,436,000); transportation equipment ($275,313,700); electrical machinery ($320,728,000); fabricated metal products ($43,654,000); stone, clay, and glass products ($117,940,000); furniture and fixtures ($209,902,500); textile mill products ($70,096,

000); printing and publishing ($48,925,000); machinery, except electrical ($204,525,000). Primary metal industries have some producers, but account for only a small part of the total.

An interesting operation in Mississippi was announced by the National Aeronautics and Space Administration in 1961. About 5 square miles (about 12.9 square kilometers) in Hancock and Pearl River counties in Mississippi and St. Tammany Parish in Louisiana were acquired for four test positions of Saturn V Apollo moon rockets. By 1967 test stands were built around a canal system, linked with the Gulf of Mexico by the Pearl River. The huge rocket stages can be lifted directly from barges into test positions.

Supporting the four test positions are about twenty buildings, including a laboratory complex, an industrial complex, and buildings for storing rocket stages.

In another futuristic project, the Atomic Energy Commission detonated a nuclear device in a Mississippi salt dome near Hattiesburg, experimenting on the possible atomic production of chemicals and the generation of power from steam.

Less exotic mining activities in the state bring Mississippi an annual income of about $400,000,000.

Recent figures (1975) show that Mississippi is in eleventh place among all the petroleum producing states, and twelfth in natural gas. Oil was not produced in the state until the late 1930s, and today annual production exceeds 40,000,000 barrels (about 5,500,000 metric tons). There are about 2,000 producing wells in over 400 fields. The largest oil refineries are at Pascagoula.

Five gas extraction plants in the state produce gasoline, butane, propane, and related products. In recent years several chemical plants have been built to use natural gas as their major raw material, and the growth of industry using petroleum as the base for chemicals—the petrochemical industry—in the state is proceeding rapidly.

Sand and gravel and cement are the next minerals in order of value of production in Mississippi. Clays for pottery and china as well as brick and tile; bentonite, used in bleaching and other chemical processes; bauxite and other aluminum ores; as well as building stones; are all produced in the state.

Industrial employers in Mississippi are quick to praise the quality of Mississippi labor. As one of them put it, "The production of one of our Mississippi plants as compared to our older Midwestern plant was 15 to 18 percent better and the quality of the work from eight to 10 percent better . . . the earnings per employee at our Mississippi plant were higher than those in our Midwestern plant due to greater efficiency."

RICHES FROM THE SEA

Mississippi's seafood and fishing industry on the Gulf Coast is of growing importance to the state and the nation. About 12,000 persons are employed, and more than 1,800 boats are used in this work. Oysters, shrimp, tuna, and flounder are among the seafoods taken and processed. The annual harvest of oysters is approximately 325,000 barrels (about 52,000 kiloliters) and the annual catch of shrimp is about 27 million pounds (about 12,000 metric tons).

Oyster and shrimp fishing, packing, and processing are especially important at Biloxi and Pascagoula. Pass Christian is particularly known for its small but delicious oysters.

In addition to processing of seafood, the state's marine industry produces cat and mink food, fish oils, meals, and vitamins. Some industrial use is being made of seawater on Mississippi's Gulf Coast by extracting minerals, notably magnesium. The state's Gulf Coast Research Laboratory is constantly working for improved use of the entire marine resources of the state.

TRANSPORTATION AND COMMUNICATION

The many rivers were the earliest and easiest means of transportation in what is now Mississippi. In the late eighteenth and early nineteenth centuries, the Mississippi was sometimes crowded with flatboats carrying the goods and produce of Ohio and Mississippi river states as far away as Pennsylvania. These were manned by rough and often rowdy men who took their cargoes generally as far as New Orleans. There the flatboats would be broken up for lumber and the men would return overland. At Natchez the flatboats sometimes tied up 14 deep.

The *New Orleans,* first steamboat on the Ohio and Mississippi rivers, started the great era of steamboating. At its height, thousands of steamboats went up not only the Mississippi but innumerable tributaries and other rivers. Steamboats were built so that they could float on shallow rivers. Every kind of steamboat was found on the river, many with the most unbelievable luxury for passengers. There were beautifully furnished lounges, bars, libraries, and game rooms. The best food was served and some passenger boats even published their own newspapers on board. More than a thousand gamblers plied their "trade" on the steamboats, fleecing unwary passengers.

The steamboat declined, but with the coming of the diesel towboats, each pushing many barges, river traffic came back stronger than ever. Special-purpose barges handle all sorts of bulk cargo—chemicals, petrochemicals, grain, minerals, and many others. Greenville, Vicksburg, and Natchez remain as major Mississippi river ports. The lower Mississippi River moves more than 100,000,000 tons (about 91,000,000 metric tons) of freight each year. The Yazoo and Pearl rivers also are open to barge traffic.

Mississippi has a particularly strategic location for travel and shipment to all of Latin America. Gulfport is the world's largest banana terminal. Owned by the state, Gulfport's banana cranes can discharge 16,000 boxes an hour.

Pascagoula is Mississippi's largest ocean port, including two deep-water harbors, grain elevators, warehouses, and industrial sites.

Adding to the state's shipping potential is its accessibility to the great coastal waterways system.

Biloxi is not considered an ocean port, but both Pascagoula and Biloxi are noted for shipbuilding. Pascagoula boatyards make a famous craft known as the lugger, and the Biloxi catboat is famous among seafarers. The Ingalls Shipyard at Pascagoula has been building ocean-going vessels since the start of World War II, and has been constructing atomic-powered submarines for the navy.

Ingall's shipyard at Pascagoula

Railroads in Mississippi were started for the purpose of feeding cotton and other products from inland communities to the rivers, where the products were transferred to steamboats. In 1831 the State Legislature chartered a railroad to run from Francisville, Louisiana, on the Mississippi, to Woodville. This was the first in Mississippi and the fifth in the entire United States to be chartered. The first rails were hewn by slaves from heart of pine, cypress, or cedar wood. The West Feliciana Railroad was the first standard-gauge railroad in the United States.

One of the world's most famous and historic pathways crosses Mississippi almost diagonally for 316 miles (about 509 kilometers) from the northeast corner to Natchez. This is the renowned Natchez Trace, the word trace meaning a line of footprints. For generations it was scarcely more than a line of footprints in many places.

The trace began far back in prehistoric times when the line of footprints was established by the buffalo and other heavy beasts. Prehistoric peoples probably used it, and the Indians found it one of the most useful means of moving across the country. European explorers and settlers found it almost as useful. The feet of de Soto, Tecumseh, Andrew Jackson, others of fame as well as soldiers of the rank, missionaries, and traders, all trudged their tiresome way along the Natchez Trace.

The American government negotiated with the Indians for rights to use the trace, with the Indians retaining the inn and ferry concessions, and the government did some work to improve the trace, but it still was hard going. For many years travelers moved in constant terror of bandits and outlaws. One of the outstanding uses of the trace was by flatboat men, who left their boats and cargoes at New Orleans and came back over the Trace through Mississippi and Tennessee, where the Trace ended at Nashville, on their way back to the upper Ohio for another boat and another cargo.

In 1938 the Federal government established the Natchez Trace Parkway. Since that time the road has been improved as a scenic and historic highway. Today, travellers can follow almost the entire length of the Trace on a fine modern highway "tracing" much of the original route closely.

Other historic routes crossed Mississippi. Across southern Mississippi ran the King's Highway, a Spanish trail connecting the Spanish possessions in Florida with those on the other side of the continent in California. The road suggested by Andrew Jackson after the difficulties he had experienced in moving men and supplies for the Creek War and the War of 1812 came to be known as the Jackson Military Road. It was authorized by Congress in 1816 and completed in the 1820s. At one time the Gaines Trace almost rivaled the Natchez Trace. The Tree Chopped Way was the trail followed by settlers moving from the eastern seaboard to Mississippi Territory.

As in most parts of the country, roads in Mississippi were rather neglected until the automobile made better roads necessary. Today Mississippi has a fine modern highway network, topped by four great swaths of the Interstate Highway system.

A network of publicly-owned and operated airports has been built throughout the state, and many privately-owned facilities. Jackson's multi-million dollar jet airport and terminal is capable of handling most commercial planes in service today, and more than a dozen Mississippi cities enjoy commercial air passenger service.

The Mississippi *Gazette,* published at Natchez in 1800, was the first newspaper of the state, but the Woodville *Republican,* begun in 1812, is the oldest newspaper still remaining in publication in Mississippi. Newspapers flourished in early Mississippi, in spite of perils to the editors, who were courageous and sometimes foolhardy in what they said, words quickly leading to action in duels. The first five editors of the Vicksburg *Sentinel* met violent deaths in a period of twenty-two years. However, newspapermen such as Alexander McClung became nationally famous. McClung was noted for his editorials on such subjects as the tariff and the national bank.

The Natchez-Vidalia Bridge spans the Mississippi at Natchez.

Old Courthouse Museum, a pre-Civil War building, on the bluffs of Vicksburg overlooking the Mississippi.

Human Treasures

JEFFERSON DAVIS

Jefferson Davis was born in Kentucky, but he spent his boyhood at Rosemont plantation near Woodville; his mother and two sisters are buried in the grounds near the house. After he graduated from West Point in 1828, he served in the Black Hawk War, then resigned his commission in 1835. He married Zachary Taylor's daughter, who died only three months after the ceremony.

Davis became a Mississippi planter and entered politics. He was elected to Congress, from which he resigned to become an officer, Colonel of the First Mississippi Regiment, in the war with Mexico. One of the high points of Jackson's history was the triumphant return of Jefferson Davis to the capital from the American triumphs in Mexico where he spoke to a huge and enthusiastic crowd.

President Franklin Pierce selected Jefferson Davis as Secretary of War, and he did much to strengthen the army and improve the defenses of the coast. He also supervised the surveying of a possible southern route for the proposed transcontinental railroad. Then he served the state and the Federal government as a United States Senator from 1857 until 1861, when he resigned immediately after Mississippi seceded.

He was elected president of the Confederate States of America for a six-year term. Many military leaders of the South felt that his interference in military matters was unwise.

After the fall of Richmond, Jefferson Davis moved his capital to Danville, Virginia, and then to Greensboro, North Carolina. During a final cabinet meeting at Charlotte, North Carolina, he informed his advisers that the Confederacy had fallen. Attempting to make his way out of the country, Davis was captured by Federal troops at Irwinville, Georgia, imprisoned at Fort Monroe, indicted for treason and then released on bail the next year. Later the trial was dropped.

Jefferson Davis traveled abroad for some time, then returned to make his home at Beauvoir, Mississippi; he lived a quiet life in the state, much revered by the people of the South. In his later years he wrote *The Rise and Fall of the Confederate Government.*

He made his last public appearance at Jackson in 1884 and died five years later on a visit to New Orleans, Louisiana. During his later years he had the devoted care of his second wife and his daughter Varina Anne Davis.

CREATIVE MISSISSIPPIANS

William Faulkner was born at New Albany in 1897. During World War I he was a pilot in the Royal Canadian Air Force and then attended the University of Mississippi. Within a few years he became known for the novels and short stories which were to make him world famous; some have called him America's most distinguished man of letters.

The Nobel Prize for literature, 1949, was awarded to William Faulkner, and the Pulitzer Prize in 1955 and 1963.

Most of his work deals with people in imaginary Yoknapatawpha County, in northern Mississippi. Actually Oxford was the setting for much of his fiction. Through his work run the stories of the lives of families of his imagined locale — the McCaslins, Compsons, Sartoris, Snopses, and others. The writing carries the region from early days of the frontier to modern industrial days. His works include *The Sound and the Fury; As I Lay Dying; Sanctuary; Absalom, Absalom!; The Unvanquished; Intruder in the Dust; Knight's Gambit; Collected Stories; Requiem for a Nun; A Fable;* and *The Reivers.*

William Faulkner died at Oxford on July 6, 1962. He has been called the finest regional interpreter who ever wrote. When Faulkner accepted the Nobel Prize in Sweden on December 10, 1950, he said of his art, revealing his philosophy: "It is his (the poet's or writer's) privilege to help man endure by lifting the heart, by reminding him of the courage and honor and hope and pride and compassion and pity and sacrifice which have been the glory of his past. The poet's voice need not merely be the record of man, it can be one of the props, the pillars to help him endure and prevail."

Eudora Welty, often called the first lady of letters in America, is one of Mississippi's most distinguished authors. She won the O. Henry Memorial Award three times, for the best American short story, and received a Guggenheim Fellowship twice. In 1952 she was elected to the National Institute of Arts and Letters. In 1954 her novel, *The Ponder Heart,* won the William Dean Howells Medal of the American Academy of Arts and Letters. She has been an honorary consultant to the Library of Congress, and writer-in-residence at several colleges, including Smith, Wellesley, and Millsaps. Among other literary awards, she has received the Lucy Donnelly Fellowship Award from Bryn Mawr, the Ingram Memorial Foundation Award, and the Bellaman Foundations Award. Among her publications, her best-known collections of short stories are *The Wide Net* and *A Curtain of Green.* Two of her novels are *Delta Wedding* and *The Ponder Heart.* In 1967 she was awarded the first Hollins Medal for Literature. She had received the Brandeis University Creative Arts Award the previous year.

The man known as Mississippi's greatest poet was Irwin Russell. He brought literary fame to Mississippi with his *Christmas Night in the Quarters.* If Russell had not died at the age of twenty-six, he might have become one of the most widely recognized names of American literature. His work is receiving considerably more attention at the present time than ever before.

Another well-known Mississippi writer was William Alexander Percy. "Planter, soldier, lawyer, cosmopolitan, and patriot—he thought of himself first and foremost as a poet." His autobiography, *Lanterns on the Levee,* has been reprinted seventeen times since it appeared in 1941 and is widely admired as an expression of the best in the Southern aristocratic tradition. Walker Percy, a relative, is a successful novelist whose first book was *The Moviegoer.*

Among popular writers, one of the best-known names for many years was Dorothy Dix, whose column of advice was read by millions. She made Pass Christian her summer home.

The artist Theora Hamblett has been compared to Grandma Moses in style. Other leading artists include Marie Hull and Karl and Mildred Wolfe.

Perhaps the best-known composer of Mississippi is the modern symphonic master William Grant Still of Woodville, whose most prominent work is the *Afro-American Symphony.* His *Song of a New Race* (Symphony in G Minor) was first performed by the Philadelphia Symphony in 1937.

Others prominent in music or theatre who have been associated with Mississippi are opera luminary Leontyne Price of Laurel, Van Cliburn, the distinguished composer-conductor, Lehman Engel, and Elvis Presley.

OTHERS IN THE PUBLIC EYE

A leading figure in the politics of his state for a long period was John Sharp Williams of Yazoo City, who served as United States Senator for twenty-five years. His wit and personality were captured in the book *An Old Fashioned Senator,* an account of his life.

A long-time United States Senator in the "Southern demagogic tradition" was Senator Theodore Bilbo of Poplarville, at one time a Baptist minister. He also served as lieutenant governor and twice as governor of Mississippi.

Another long-popular figure was Edward Cary Walthal of Holly Springs, who served four terms as a United States Senator.

In the governor's chair, the first native-born chief executive of the state was Gerard C. Brandon, of near Washington. Modern Governor Paul B. Johnson, inaugurated January 21, 1964, is a member of a distinguished political family. His father, Paul B. Johnson, Sr., served as governor of Mississippi from 1940 until his death in 1943.

An outstanding woman in the political life of the state was Ellen Sullivan Woodward, member of the State Board of Development, State Research Commission, State Board of Public Welfare, head of the women's division of the Federal Works Progress Administration, and only woman assistant administrator in the program.

Among the state's military leaders were thirty-four generals in the Confederate army. A hero not only of the Civil War but also of the Seminole War, the war with Mexico, and the Comanche wars was

General Earl Van Dorn. Earlier military heroes were General John A. Quitman, hero of the Mexican War, said to be one of the most popular men in America at the time of his death, also a governor of Mississippi and congressman; and David Farragut, America's first admiral, whose boyhood home was near Pascagoula.

Business leaders include Gail Borden, who grew up in Liberty and produced the first successful condensed milk; William Dunbar, first to find the usefulness of cottonseed oil; and Lamont Rowlands, who brought the culture of tung nuts into the region.

One of the outstanding Indian leaders of America was Greenwood Leflore, last chief of the Choctaw, who never ceased working for his people. He persuaded the government to give the Indians many additional benefits in the treaty that sent the Indians to Oklahoma, but his people never forgave him for urging them to accept the government offer. He remained in Mississippi and became a successful planter. Another outstanding Choctaw chief was Mashulatubbee, also a wealthy man, who was one of the strongest opponents of the Treaty of Dancing Rabbit.

SUCH INTERESTING PEOPLE

One of the more unusual men in American history was Revolutionary General James Wilkinson. He was involved in many unpopular events, such as the plot to remove General Washington from command during the Revolutionary War, the Spanish conspiracy, and the Burr affair. He was also charged with treasonable relations with Spain in 1811. Each time he seemed to come out in the clear and with a better reputation than ever. He had the friendship of Washington, Hamilton, Jefferson, and Adams, and they all defended him. However, Spanish records reveal that Wilkinson was in the pay of Spain while a general in the United States Army. A letter written by General Wilkinson is said to have been the basis for *The Man Without a Country* by Edward Everett Hale.

Sam Dale of Daleville had an exciting life. As a boy he learned the Indian methods of warfare and became an Indian trader. In the War of 1812 he is said to have killed seven Indians in one war canoe. He delivered dispatches to General Andrew Jackson from Georgia to Madisonville, Louisiana, in only seven and a half days, and he and his horse returned after resting only one night. Dale helped supervise the removal of the Choctaw to Oklahoma. When he died, Chief Leflore said, "Big Chief, you sleep here, but your spirit is a brave and a chieftain in the hunting grounds of the sky." In October, 1967 a statue and park were dedicated in his honor at Daleville.

Bravery of another type was shown by Betsy Allen, a Chickasaw Indian woman. When her husband tried to take her Indian slave, she carried the case to the United States Supreme Court and won. The matter was given little thought until about a hundred years later when Betsy Allen was "rediscovered" as being the first woman in the United States to whom the rights of property had been guaranteed.

Other prominent Mississippi women include Eliza Jane Poitevent of Pearl Rivers, who was one of the first women to manage a newspaper successfully (Dorothy Dix was her protege); Madeline Price of near Natchez, who was courted by Aaron Burr; Jane Long, who is known as "The Mother of Texas"; Kate Jones Thompson, who so pleased Queen Victoria of England that she gave her a gold and dia-

Choctaw Indian children during recess.

mond thimble; Grace McManus, artist, who was chosen to hand illuminate the prayer books given out to celebrate the coronation of King Edward VII of England; and Eliza Moore of Red Banks, who defied Union soldiers to save her home.

One of the strangest of all experiences was that of Will Purvis, convicted of murder, although most of the state thought he was innocent. When he was hanged, the rope slipped from his neck; so many saw this as a sign of innocence that he was saved from hanging and sent to jail. After fifteen horrible years, another man confessed to the murder and Will Purvis went free. He lived on as a farmer, with the scars of the noose on his neck.

Another different but also strange story was that of the handsome Cox family, the five sons of William Henry Cox who came to live on their father's land, named Galena, near Holly Springs. All five died tragically. William Henry, Jr., rode his horse up a stairway and broke his neck. Toby killed his bride and then committed suicide. Another brother plunged over a bluff in a wagon as he was driving a pair of horses at full speed. William Henry Jr.'s daughter inherited the great estate.

A family history of an entirely different type was that of the Percys of Greenville. Colonel William Alexander Percy was a leader of his fellow Mississippians during Reconstruction days. His son was Senator LeRoy Percy. The grandson was William Alexander Percy, lawyer and poet. The Percy home at Greenville had a fine art collection, including five pieces of sculpture by renowned Jacob Epstein.

Judge Robert A. Hill of Oxford was opposed to secession and took no part in the war; however, his integrity was so respected that he continued to be highly regarded by both sides. This was also true of Judge William L. Sharkey, who was appointed provisional governor. At the close of the war they were able to do more than almost any others to bring both sides back together.

Another notable Mississippi judge was Judge Edward McGehee, whose career, typical of the best elements of the Natchez planters life, was told by Stark Young in the book *So Red the Rose*. Judge McGehee financed the West Feliciana Railroad and gave a high tone to the life of Natchez, which still remembers his influence.

University Medical Center at Jackson.

Teaching and Learning

There are eight universities and eight four-year colleges in Mississippi today. In 1802 the first higher education institution to be chartered in the old Southeast was incorporated—Jefferson College at Washington. One of its most famous faculty members was John James Audubon, the naturalist-artist.

The University of Mississippi was founded in 1844, with Oxford winning the site by one vote in the legislature. The university opened in 1848, and James A. Ventress was known as the "Father of the University." After closing during the Civil War, the university was reopened. Today its student body numbers about 8,500. The university is known for medical work. In 1961 a university surgical team successfully completed the first operation ever performed on a human being under electrical anesthesia. The Forest Products Laboratory is another noted division of the university.

Mississippi State University at State College, founded in 1878, now has a larger enrollment than the University of Mississippi and the University of Southern Mississippi at Hattiesburg, founded in 1910, is the largest. Mississippi State College for Women, Columbus, was the first state-supported university for women in the country. Other state universities are Delta State, Cleveland; Jackson State; Mississippi Valley, Itta Bena; and Alcorn State, Lorman.

Other Mississippi colleges are Belhaven and Millsaps, Jackson; Blue Mountain; Mississippi College, Clinton; Rust, Holly Springs; Tougaloo; and William Carey, Hattiesburg.

Mississippi claims to be the first state in the nation to have a planned state system of junior colleges. There are nearly thirty public and private junior colleges in the state.

Efforts were made to set up schools in Mississippi as early as 1772, and many private schools were established over the years. The first free school in Mississippi was Franklin Academy, Columbus. In 1846 an act for a general school system was passed, and a uniform system of public education was established in 1870.

In the tremendously important field of research, Mississippi established the Research and Development Center at Jackson to perform

Above: The Lycean Building at the University of Mississippi. Below: An informal outdoor class.

research and plan functions in support of state, area, and local action agencies. This institution, a part of the Mississippi Universities Center complex, is designed to strengthen the sciences and fundamental research in other institutions of higher learning and coordinate all applied research relating to economic development. Although working closely with other institutions, the center is completely independent of them.

Another important phase of education in Mississippi today is the program of vocational and technical training, established under Governor Paul B. Johnson, for setting up vocational and technical training centers at the state's junior colleges.

The coast of Mississippi provides a vast recreational resource.

Enchantment of Mississippi

Tourists spend more than $400,000,000 each year in Mississippi in their visits to the "Hospitality State."

JACKSON

Louis Le Fleur made a journey of exploration up the Pearl River and was so impressed with the perfect location for a post on the bluffs of the river that he set up his trading post on what came to be known as Le Fleur's Bluff.

Today that location is known as Jackson, the thriving capital of Mississippi, scene of much of the history of the state.

The massive capitol was authorized in 1900 and opened in June, 1903, at a cost of $1,000,000, towering over the city on a high terrace. At the top of the central dome and its lantern is the symbol of America, a great copper eagle, covered with gold leaf.

Not only does this capitol resemble the national capitol, but the governor's mansion is much like the White House in appearance. It also occupies grounds covering an entire block.

One of Mississippi's most prized structures is the Old Capitol Building. Here the state's idol, Andrew Jackson, once addressed the people, and in its storied halls much of the history of the state was written. In 1961 Mississippi spent nearly $2,000,000 to restore the Old Capitol, under the supervision of the State Department of Archives and History. This department, started in 1902, was the second established in the United States, and has been a model for many similar departments in other states. The Old Capitol now houses the State Historical Museum. One of its finest exhibits is the state Hall of Fame's portraits of prominent Mississippians.

The Archives and History Building was completed in 1969, and the Museum of Natural Science is considered to be one of the finest in the South.

The State Wildlife Museum has a collection of more than 21,000 specimens, a large display of Mississippi animal life. Living creatures and trees and floral displays, including Japanese and tropical gardens, are found at Mynelle Gardens. Not far from Jackson is Mississippi Petrified Forest, with a museum and dioramas.

After the Jackson Municipal Art Gallery burned, a new Arts Museum and planetarium was constructed. One of the few remaining plantation homes in the Jackson region is Sub Rosa Plantation, restored and furnished with fine antiques. The campuses of five colleges add to the points of interest in the Jackson area.

In 1965 the first Mississippi Arts Festival was held at Jackson. The four-day event brought internationally famous artists, such as Van Cliburn and the New Christy Minstrels, and attractions such as the New York City Ballet. It also honored Mississippi authors and artists. So successful was the festival, with over seventy-five thousand in attendance, that it has become an annual event of Jackson.

Many Mississippians are active in art, with art colonies at Stafford Springs, near Laurel, Pascagoula, and Jackson. Marie Hull's classes at Jackson draw students of all ages.

NATCHEZ

A visit to Natchez in March or April might convince a stranger that the city had never left the plantation days before the Civil War,

Longwood, a mansion in the Natchez region.

as men in morning coats and beautiful girls stroll the grounds of elegant houses. This, of course, is the famed Natchez Pilgrimage, in which many of the finest homes and gardens are opened to visitors. However, much of the time Natchez still appears to be a museum of the past, and many of the homes and gardens are open all year.

At one time Natchez was the last point of civilization in the southeast. The Spanish built magnificent structures, only a few of which remain in the old Spanish section. The Elms, built in 1783, is one of the few Spanish mansions still occupied as a residence. In the heyday of the planters, Natchez was the capital of an unparalleled culture built by aristocratic people who created a new kind of civilization.

Many of the plantation houses remain. Perhaps typical of these was D'Evereux, approached by a winding drive, crossing and recrossing through the woodland. Bordering the drive were hedges of Cherokee rose and other ornamental plants.

Another mansion of the Natchez region, one of the best known in the South, is Longwood. Rising six stories, it was built in octagonal shape, and was never finished, due to the Civil War. Its thirty-two eight-sided rooms and huge onion-shaped copper dome are distinctive features. Each room had niches to hold the classic statuary from Italy and Greece. Fireplaces were made from Italian marble.

Still another mansion of note near Natchez is Springfield, where Andrew Jackson is said to have been married.

One of the remarkable buildings in Natchez is Connelly's Tavern. Here the swarms of river boatmen were entertained, along with the Duke of Orleans and many other famous persons. Here, it is said, Aaron Burr and Blennerhassett met to discuss their mysterious schemes, and the American flag was raised for the first time in the lower Mississippi Valley. The historic structure has been restored and refurnished and is operated by the Natchez Garden Club. Stanton Hall, one of the great Natchez mansions, has been restored and is operated by the Pilgrimage Garden Club.

Among the city's churches, one of the most notable is St. Mary's Cathedral. Prince Alex Torlonia of Rome donated the bell, and as it was being cast, the princess, his wife, threw her wedding ring into the molten metal to improve the tone and bring good luck.

VICKSBURG

Memories of the terrible siege and battles through which Vicksburg suffered still cast their shadow on this historic city—the first ever to experience what might be called the total war of modern times.

When Congress established the Vicksburg National Military Park and Cemetery, the act read, "to commemorate the Campaign, Siege and Defense of Vicksburg and to preserve the history of the battles and operations on the ground where they were fought." This has been done so well that the visitor can learn the whole plan and history of the war around the city from the layout of the park, from the monuments and from the museum exhibits. The museum also contains interesting items taken from the Union gunboat *Cairo,* sunk in the Yazoo River during the war. In the park are twenty-three regimental markers as well as the monuments raised by many states whose boys took part in the engagement. Some of these monuments are magnificent. Among the most outstanding are the Mississippi, Iowa, and Illinois monuments in the park.

Of those who died, more than 17,000 Union soldiers rest in the military cemetery, almost 13,000 of them unidentified.

The largest stern-wheeler ever built was the steamer *Sprague.* It was known affectionately as "Big Mama" by river people and set many records for passenger and towing transportation. It was used in 1950 as the setting for the motion picture *Show Boat.* Until it burned, it was tied to the Vicksburg dock, and was used as a living museum of the picturesque steamboat days.

The Old Court House at Vicksburg has been restored and now is a museum, supposed to house the largest collection of Confederate materials in the country. Other displays show Indian, pioneer, and related items. Over the building, Grant raised the United States flag, signaling the end of his ferocious siege of that city which lasted forty-seven days.

The United States Waterways Experiment Station houses models of rivers, locks, harbors, dams, and tidal waterways for study of flood control, navigation, and harbor problems.

*Old Fort
Massachusetts*

One such problem was solved by a little Vicksburg boy. In 1876, Vicksburg, which had been an important port, was landlocked by a sudden change of the Mississippi River. The city seemed to be doomed, as so many others have been when the Mississippi moved away. However, in 1902 a young Vicksburg boy suggested how the Yazoo River might be changed to bring the river back to Vicksburg. Government engineers closed the mouth of the Yazoo, and dug a canal to turn the Yazoo waters into the old channel of the Mississippi, restoring Vicksburg's port.

AMERICA'S RIVIERA—THE GULF COAST

The Old Spanish Fort, built in 1718 by the French and later captured by the Spanish, may still be seen at Pascagoula, with its massive 18-inch (about 46 centimeters) walls formed of heavy timbers and cemented with oyster shells and mud and moss. It is said to be the oldest remaining fort in the Mississippi Valley.

The mysterious Singing River can best be heard at twilight during the warmest summer days. No one has solved the mystery of its "musical sound." Another mystery of the Pascagoula region is the disappearance of the Pascagoula Indians from which the city and river get their names.

Ocean Springs, site of old Biloxi, is the oldest permanent settlement in Mississippi.

Biloxi, over which eight flags have flown, has been popular as a resort since 1840. The bloom of magnolia, camellias, roses, and

81

crepe myrtle, and the many outdoor pleasures of the 25 miles (about 40 kilometers) of beaches all add to the city's attractions.

One of America's historic structures is the old Biloxi Lighthouse, built in 1848. Citizens painted it black when Abraham Lincoln was assassinated. Now automatic, in earlier days the lighthouse had two keepers, mother and daughter—Maria and Miranda Younghans—who served the government and seafaring people for sixty-two years.

Nearby Ship and Deer islands are steeped in history and lore, as are the other barrier islands. Fort Massachusetts on Ship Island was used as a Civil War prison.

Between Biloxi and Gulfport is Beauvoir House, last home of Confederate President Jefferson Davis, now completely restored as a permanent Confederate shrine, with authentic furnishings and a museum showing the family's personal effects. One of the state's finest resorts is Gulf Hills, a showplace near Biloxi.

Gulfport was a planned city, laid out in straight lines parallel to the sea wall. One of the major attractions of the coast is Marine Life Oceanarium at Gulfport.

At Long Beach, with its almost 5 miles (about 8 kilometers) of sand beach, in earlier days the poet Vachel Lindsay held his college classes on a platform tucked in the branches of a huge live oak.

Old Biloxi lighthouse

The Shrimp Festival is the first week in June.

Pass Christian is named for adjoining Christian Pass. The longtime resort city has been host to Presidents Jackson, Taylor, Grant, T. Roosevelt, Wilson, and Truman. Offshore is the world's largest oyster reef.

So many countries have controlled Bay St. Louis, a famed resort, that twenty-three different types of land tenure have been recognized there. The Church of Our Lady of the Gulf is the seat of the state's largest Catholic parish.

At Waveland is Pirates' House, once the home of a businessman from New Orleans, who is said to have been the secret boss of the entire group of Gulf of Mexico pirates.

OTHER POINTS OF INTEREST

Near the 500,420-acre (about 200,000 hectares) De Soto National Forest, Hattiesburg still is a center for lumber and naval stores, but other industries have added prosperity to the region. The city is also the educational center of its area, with the large and thriving University of Southern Mississippi and William Carey College. Paul B. Johnson State Park is nearby. The well-known South Mississippi Gun and Dog Club Field Trials are held each year in the national forest.

Laurel is a notable center of culture, especially for a city of its size. Its Lauren Rogers Library and Museum of Art—first art museum in the state—is one of the finest small museums in the country. Its art collection includes such masters as Constable, Inness, Millet, Whistler, Reynolds, and Rousseau, fine Chinese and Japanese collections, and an excellent collection of basketry and statuary.

The forward-looking plans of the Eastman-Gardiner Lumber Company encouraged lumber workers to buy their homes as well as pianos and other fine things and helped Laurel to thrive when other lumber towns were dying. The pioneer hardboard plant of Masonite, the parent plant of this large corporation, is located at Laurel.

Meridian is a center for livestock and farm marketing as well as industry. The only naval air station in the state is nearby; here all Navy and Marine Corps aviators take their first solo jet flights. Meridian is known for its annual Lively Arts Festival in February, featuring children's programs, art exhibits, plays, and concerts.

The nation's first observance of Decoration Day (now called Memorial Day) was held at Columbus in April, 1863, when the women of the city gathered at Friendship Cemetery and placed decorations of flowers on the graves of both Confederate and Union soldiers who were buried there. The first formal observance of Decoration Day was held there on April 25, 1866. In Jackson, formal observance was held on April 26, 1866, and April 26 was observed as Confederate Memorial Day in Mississippi until the 1966 session of the legislature designated it to be April 25, at the request of the people of Columbus and Loundes County. Columbus, on three rivers—

Tombigbee, Luxapalia, and Buttahatchie—has matured from a trading post to a center of education, which has set many of the traditions of the old South. The Indians thought the town's first tavern keeper looked like an old opossum, so the community was first known as Possum Town. Later, the planters built impressive homes, and more than a hundred of them may still be seen in tours which are available. The Strategic Air Command jet training program is carried on at nearby Columbus Air Force Base.

Tupelo was the first city in the country to sign up for power from the Tennessee Valley Authority. The less expensive electricity has been responsible for much of the city's industrial growth. In the Chickasaw language, the word Tupelo means lodging place, and the region was once the lodging place of a large group of Chickasaw.

At Tupelo is one of the first Federal fish hatcheries, distributing about 3,000,000 fish per year. Near Tupelo on the Natchez Trace Parkway is Chickasaw Village and Ackia Battleground, where two separate French forces were defeated by the Chickasaw.

Other memories of French battles with the Indians are preserved at Pontotoc, heart of the Chickasaw country. A marker tells of Father Antoine Senat who chose to be burned at the stake with twenty French companions rather than escape because he was a priest. In some rocks of the cliffs in the vicinity may be seen the holes in which Chickasaw women ground their corn.

The site of Brice's Crossroads Battle near Baldwyn has been made a national battlefield. Here Confederate General Nathan Bedford Forrest enjoyed one of his greatest successes, against a much larger force of Union men.

The mineral springs of Iuka were first used by the Indians and then became popular with white settlers. The town is the location of another important Civil War battle.

Clarksdale took its name from the Englishman who laid it out, John Clark. Nearby Sunflower Landing is one of the locations where De Soto is said to have discovered the Mississippi River. The precise spot has never been known for sure. Clarksdale relishes its nickname as the "Golden Buckle of the Cotton Belt," and it is the center of one of the richest cotton areas.

Loading cotton onto barges.

A still richer cotton area is centered on Greenwood, one of the world's great cotton markets. John Williams bought 162 acres (about 66 hectares) of land for $1.25 per acre, and built a river boat landing on the Yazoo. Chief Greenwood Leflore tried to set up a competitive cotton shipping point but the Williams landing won out and became the prosperous city which took the chief's first name of Greenwood.

Located on the eastern fringe of the delta, Grenada is also dependent on cotton for much of its business. The city was once two very independent and quarrelsome towns, but became united in 1836. The unity was symbolized by a wedding with the bride coming from one town and the groom from the other. Near the city are Carver Point and Hugh White state parks and Grenada Lake.

The largest river port in Mississippi is Greenville. Through much of its history Greenville paid for its importance on the river as the Mississippi currents ate away huge chunks of the city which periodically dropped into the water. In 1927 the whole town was below water for seventy days. In 1935 levees were built to force the river six miles (about 10 kilometers) to the west, and a new harbor and terminal were finished in 1957 on Lake Ferguson, now a placid expanse of water, opening into the river to the south of Greenville.

Another $3,000,000 improvement to this harbor was finished in 1963. The city is home port for over forty privately-owned towing, marine building, and upkeep companies. They operate dozens of towboats, and grain, oil, and other barges.

Greenville has long been known as a literary center. The *Delta Review*, an outstanding literary magazine, is published here, and writers William Alexander Percy, David Cohn, Shelby Foote, Louise Crump, Ellen Douglas, and Hodding Carter have lived here.

Goodman is particularly interesting to large numbers of Masonic and Eastern Star members. In the Little Red School near Goodman, founded by Masons of the Goodman region, Robert Morris had the idea for the Order of the Eastern Star and wrote much of the ritual of the order there.

Port Gibson is the Mississippi town which General U. S. Grant would not destroy because he said it was "too beautiful to burn." Nearby is the Grand Gulf Museum and Park, where Civil War earthworks are still plainly visible. A number of the business buildings in Port Gibson date from 1840 or earlier, and there are many examples of antebellum plantation cottages in the residential section. Old Wintergreen cemetery has been called the most beautiful in the state.

Raymond is a town in which Andrew Jackson once spoke and the great admiration felt by the people of Mississippi for Jackson is shown by the fact that after his speech the residents laid linen sheets on the boardwalks in Jackson's path as a mark of respect.

The area of Washington has many memories of the strange affairs of Aaron Burr. Calverton Plantation, southeast of Natchez, was the scene where Governor Mead of Mississippi met Aaron Burr and took him into custody to be tried, and the trial took place at Washington in the shadows of the Burr Oaks at Jefferson College campus. Tiny Washington at one time was the capital of Mississippi.

McComb is celebrated for its azaleas, but the McComb azalea festival is different from those of other cities. The people have given great attention to lighting their azaleas, and at night the azalea trail of McComb is a fairyland of light and bloom.

Picayune adjoins the National Aeronautics and Space Administration's National Space Technology Laboratories. The city also was the

Windsor, a handsome estate built in 1860, was destroyed by a fire in 1890.

center of the state's tung orchards until most of them were destroyed by hurricane.

These activities give evidence of the rapid changes in many fields, through which Mississippi is taking its place in the modern age.

Handy Reference Section

Instant Facts

Became the 20th state December 10, 1817
Capital—Jackson, founded 1821
Nickname—Magnolia State
State Motto— *Virtute et Armis* (By valor and arms)
State Bird—Mockingbird
State Flower—Magnolia blossom
State Tree—Magnolia
State Song—"Go, Mississippi," words and music by Houston Davis
Area—47,716 square miles (123,583.9 square kilometers)
Rank in area—31st
Coastline—44 miles (70.8 kilometers)
Shoreline—359 miles (577.8 kilometers)
Greatest Length (north to south)—340 miles (547.2 kilometers)
Greatest Width (east to west)—180 miles (289.7 kilometers)
Highest Point—806 feet (245.7 meters), Woodall Mountain, Tishomingo
          County
Lowest Point—Sea level
Geographic Center—Leake, 9 miles (14.4 kilometers) w.n.w. of Carthage
Mean elevation—300 feet (91.4 meters)
Number of Counties—82
Highest Recorded Temperature—115°F, (46.1°C), Holly Springs
Lowest Recorded Temperature—minus 16°F, (26.7°C), Batesville
Population—2,700,000 (1977 estimate)
Population Rank—30th
Population Density—56.5 per square mile (21.9 per square kilometer)
Center of Population—In Leake County, 10.2 miles (16.4 kilometers) s.w.
          of Carthage
Illiteracy rate—2.4 percent
Birthrate—19.5 per 1,000
Infant mortality rate—25.2 per 1,000
Physicians per 100,000—94
Principal Cities—Jackson, 153,968
          Biloxi, 48,486
          Meridian, 45,083
          Gulfport, 40,791
          Greenville, 39,648
          Hattiesburg, 38,277
          Vicksburg, 25,478

You Have a Date with History

1541—De Soto discovers the Mississippi River
1629—King of England includes much of Mississippi in Carolina grant
1673—Marquette and Joliet come down the river
1682—La Salle explores; claims region for France
1699—Fort Maurepas (Ocean Springs) first permanent settlement in
       lower Mississippi Valley
1712—Anthony Crozat given commercial rights
1719—John Law takes over region
1729—Natchez Indian massacre, Fort Rosalie (Natchez)
1730—French attack, kill and disperse Natchez tribe
1736—Chickasaw defeat French at Ackia
1763—England gains control
1781—Spain takes over
1783—American title to northern Mississippi recognized
1795—Spain recognizes American claim to land north of 31°
1798—Territory of Mississippi organized
1802—Washington made capital
1806—Improved cotton seed from Mexico
1809—First lumber mill established
1810—Republic of West Florida established, annexed by United States
1813—Creek War
1814—Action in War of 1812
1817—Statehood—Natchez made first state capital
1821—Capital moved to Jackson
1830—By Treaty of Dancing Rabbit, Choctaw agree to removal
1832—New state constitution; Chickasaw treaty of Pontotoc provides for
       their removal
1844—University of Mississippi chartered
1861—Mississippi secedes
1862—Battles of Shiloh, Iuka, Booneville, Tallahatchie Ridge,
       Coffeeville, Holly Springs; first Decoration Day at Columbus
1863—Vicksburg, Jackson, Natchez fall
1864—Battles of Meridian, Okolona, Brice's Cross Roads, Tupelo, Egypt
1865—Provisional government appointed
1866—Legislature refuses to ratify 13th and 14th amendments
1867—Military control of state
1868—New constitution rejected
1869—Modified constitution adopted
1870—Mississippi readmitted to Union
1875—Race riots
1876—Reconstruction period ends
1878—Yellow fever epidemic
1882—Act to encourage industry

1890—Present constitution approved
1904—Planter control ends
1913—Mississippi becomes "Winter White House"
1917—World War I begins, in which 66,000 from Mississippi serve
1927—Worst Mississippi River flood
1936—Tornado kills 201 at Tupelo
1938—Natchez Trace Parkway established
1941—World War II begins, in which 202,560 from Mississippi serve;
    4,187 die
1965—Industry passes agriculture in Mississippi
1966—Prohibition terminated
1967—Rocket test center completed in Hancock County
1969—Charles Evers becomes first black mayor since Reconstruction

Governors of the State of Mississippi

David Holmes, 1817-1820
George Poindexter, 1820-1822
Walter Leake, 1822-1825
Gerard C. Brandon, 1825-1826
David Holmes, 1826
Gerald C. Brandon, 1826-1832
Abram M. Scott, 1832-1833
Charles Lynch, 1833
Hiram G. Runnels, 1833-1835
John A. Quitman, 1835-1836
Charles Lynch, 1836-1838
Alexander G. McNutt, 1838-1842
Tilgham M. Tucker, 1842-1844
Albert G. Brown, 1844-1848
Joseph M. Matthews, 1848-1850
John A. Quitman, 1850-1851
John I. Guion, 1851
James Whitfield, 1851-1852
Henry S. Foote, 1852-1854
John J. Pettus, 1854
John J. McRae, 1854-1857
Wm. McWillie, 1857-1859
John J. Pettus, 1859-1863
Charles Clark, 1863-1865
William L. Sharkey, 1865
Benjamin G. Humphreys, 1865-1868
Adelbert Ames, 1868-1870
James L. Alcorn, 1870-1871

Ridgley C. Powers, 1871-1874
Adelbert Ames, 1874-1876
John M. Stone, 1876-1882
Robert Lowry, 1882-1890
John M. Stone, 1890-1896
Anslem J. McLaurin, 1896-1900
Andrew W. Longino, 1900-1904
James Kimble Vardaman, 1904-1908
Edmond Favor Noel, 1908-1912
Earl LeRoy Brewer, 1912-1916
Theodore Gilmore Bilbo, 1916-1920
Lee Maurice Russell, 1920-1924
Henry Lewis Whitfield, 1924-1927
Dennis Murphree, 1827-1928
Theodore Gilmore Bilbo, 1928-1932
Martin Sennett Conner, 1932-1936
Hugh White, 1936-1940
Paul B. Johnson, 1940-1943
Dennis Murphree, 1943-1944
Thomas L. Bailey, 1944-1946
Fielding L. Wright, 1946-1948
Fielding L. Wright, 1948-1952
Hugh L. White, 1952-1956
J. P. Coleman, 1956-1960
Ross R. Barnett, 1960-1964
Paul B. Johnson, Jr., 1964-1968
John Bell Williams, 1968-1972
William Waller, 1972-1976
Cliff Finch, 1976-

Index

92

94

PICTURE CREDITS

ABOUT THE AUTHOR

With the publication of his first book for school use when he was twenty, **Allan Carpenter** began a career as an author that has spanned more than 135 books. After teaching in the public schools of Des Moines, Mr. Carpenter began his career as an educational publisher at the age of twenty-one when he founded the magazine *Teachers Digest*. In the field of educational periodicals, he was responsible for many innovations. During his many years in publishing, he has perfected a highly organized approach to handling large volumes of factual material: after extensive traveling and having collected all possible materials, he systematically reviews and organizes everything. From his apartment high in Chicago's John Hancock Building, Allan recalls, "My collection and assimilation of materials on the states and countries began before the publication of my first book." Allan is the founder of Carpenter Publishing House and of Infordata International, Inc., publishers of *Issues in Education* and *Index to U. S. Government Periodicals*. When he is not writing or traveling, his principal avocation is music. He has been the principal bassist of many symphonies, and he managed the country's leading non-professional symphony for twenty-five years.